Disorders of Discourse

Real Language Series

General Editors:
Jennifer Coates, Roehampton Institute, London
Jenny Cheshire, Queen Mary and Westfield College, University of London
and
Euan Reid, Institute of Education, University of London

Titles published in the series:

David Lee Competing Discourses: Perspective and Ideology in Language

Norman Fairclough (Editor) Critical Language Awareness

James Milroy and **Lesley Milroy** (Editors) Real English: The Grammar of English Dialects in the British Isles

Mark Sebba London Jamaican: Language Systems in Interaction

Janet Holmes Women, Men and Politeness

Ben Rampton Crossing: Language and Ethnicity Among Adolescence

Brian V. Street Social Literacies: Critical Approaches to Literacy in Development, Ethnography and Education

Srikant Sarangi and **Stefaan Slembrouck** Language, Bureaucracy and Social Control

Ruth Wodak Disorders of Discourse

Disorders of Discourse

Ruth Wodak

LONGMAN
LONDON AND NEW YORK

Addison Wesley Longman Limited,
Edinburgh Gate,
Harlow, Essex CM20 2JE, England
and Associated Companies throughout the world

*Published in the United States of America
by Addison Wesley Longman, New York*

First published 1996

ISBN 0 582 099579 CSD
ISBN 0 582 099560 PPR

British Library Cataloguing-in-Publication Data

A catalogue record for this book is
available from the British Library

Library of Congress Cataloging-in-Publication Data

Wodak, Ruth, 1950–
    Disorders of discourse / Ruth Wodak.
       p.   cm.–(Real language series)
    Includes bibliographical references (p.) and index.
    ISBN 0-582-09957-9. – ISBN 0-582-09956-0 (pbk.)
    1. Discourse analysis–Social aspects. 2. Sociolinguistics.
    3. Group psychotherapy. I. Title. II. Series.
    P302.84.W63   1996
    306.4 '4–dc20   95-50719
                                            CIP

Set by 33 in 10/12pt Sabon
Produced by Longman Singapore Publishers (Pte) Ltd.
Printed in Singapore

Contents

Acknowledgements

This book focuses on two areas which have formed a major part of my research activities over the past two decades. This research programme was in many ways a cumulative one, and some of the earlier studies I have drawn upon in writing this book date back several years. Given the expanse of time and the sheer number of people who have offered support and advice or helped clarify theoretical, methodological or empirical issues with me, I cannot possibly hope to acknowledge everyone who fits into the above categories. I would only ask those whose names do not appear here to forgive me my oversight, memory lapse or selection criteria; I was, and remain, exceedingly grateful to all of you, for all you have done, and will try to do justice to those whose contributions I have chosen to acknowledge explicitly.

These earlier studies which formed the empirical basis of many of the chapters in the book were funded by the following Austrian grant-giving bodies, which I most gratefully acknowledge: The Research Fund of the Austrian National Bank and the Austrian Ministry of Science and Research.

Since much of the research I have carried out in the areas of institutional discourse and of comprehension and comprehensibility as an intersection between an institution and everyday life has been collaborative, I should like to acknowledge up front my colleagues and research associates. The study on doctor–patient interaction was carried out together with Johanna Lalouschek and Florian Menz. Benedikt Lutz, who wrote his doctoral dissertation on comprehensibility, was an indispensable collaborator in the study involving the comprehension and comprehensibility of news broadcasts. Finally, the study on the school partnership was also conducted with the assistance of researchers Johanna Lalouschek, Elisabeth (Andraschko) Kriechbaum and Heidemarie Schrodt. Most of my research associates over the past years have been students or former students of mine, so it is not without a measure of pride that I emphasize the indispensability of their participation in these ambitious empirical studies.

Over the years, my colleagues at the Department of Linguistics at the University of Vienna have been an important source of intellectual stimulation. In this respect I should like to acknowledge my debt to Wolfgang Dressler and in particular to the late Jochem Schindler. Joki's recent tragic early death not only deprived the field of Indo-European languages of one of its most brilliant minds, but has also meant the loss of a rigorously analytical critic and, most importantly, also of a solicitous and understanding friend. Harald Leupold-Loewenthal and the late Hans Strotzka, both psychoanalysts and renowned scholars, were generous with their valuable advice in helping me develop an interdisciplinary framework needed for my research on language behaviour in therapy groups. More recently, I have been fortunate to be able to discuss many important theoretical issues about 'critical linguistics' with my colleagues and friends Teun van Dijk, Norman Fairclough, Theo van Leeuwen and Gunter Kress. They have been a source of invaluable knowledge of varied cultural contexts of discourse production, of theoretical rigour and of criticism of individual or collaborative work. Yet the collegial atmosphere of mutual respect in which these critical exchanges have taken place has been nearly as rewarding as the criticism itself.

The debts incurred in writing this book are more recent, though equally important. Richard Schrodt and Rudolf de Cillia each made valuable comments on drafts of several of the chapters, for which I am very grateful. Longman's series editors Jenny Cheshire and Jennifer Coates not only provided me with many useful suggestions about the book's structure and expository style, but were also extremely patient with my endless questions and general hesitation about writing a book in English. I think I would have given up long ago had I not had the benefit of John Hampson's extraordinary editorial skills. He revised almost the entire first draft of the book and made its English readable for an English-speaking audience. Lieselotte Martin has spent countless hours typing corrections to the manuscript, and has managed to keep her good humour throughout. These few words, however, cannot adequately express my gratitude to her for her tireless efforts. Naturally, I alone am responsible for the final version of the book.

Finally, I would like to thank Richard Mitten, for all the time he has spent with me, either in discussing the outline of the book, or in dealing with the many problems which popped up, and for contributing valuable ideas and comments. Without his high-level intellectual contributions and the strong emotional support he supplies I would not be able to continue my work in the way I consider important.

This book is dedicated to my son Jakob, who has had so much patience with me and lets me work, although it means that I am able to spend far less time with him than either he or I would like. Jakob hopes the book will be a bestseller, though he does seem to understand that scholarly books are not normally the kind that millions of people buy. In any event, I hope he will nevertheless be satisfied, and will still love me even if it is not.

Vienna, April 1996

1 *Introduction: orders and disorders*

1.1 Discourse sociolinguistics

1.1.1 *Stating the problems*

> The opening balance is equal to the closing balance carried forward from the last debit entry minus subsequent expenditures; however, payments for estimated personal tax liabilities (e.g. prepayments for sales tax) and payments of deducted tax contributions (e.g. income tax) as well as family assistance contributions paid by the employer, are to be excluded, unless they compensate for estimated personal tax liabilities.

This is an excerpt from the Austrian Ministry of Finance's 'Explanatory Notes' attached to its notice on taxes and expenditures.

> Patient: What did you mean about cholesterol?
> Doctor: Well, there are new guidelines, specifically those regarding HDL and LDL cholesterol. And we'll take it from you and then we'll see what happens.

This is an excerpt from a dialogue between a doctor and a patient at the outpatient clinic of a Vienna hospital.

> Austria: In February the increase in the consumer price index totalled 6 per cent in comparison to February 1981. Averaged out over the year it was thus somewhat lower than the yearly rate of inflation. It was put at 6.1 per cent by the government statistical office. In contrast, the rate of increase of consumer prices fell in the monthly comparison.

This is an excerpt from Austrian Broadcasting Company radio news, 15 February 1982.

Three everyday situations in which much depends on precise and relevant information (i.e. content) being properly and accurately conveyed: government tax guidelines, an outpatient clinic, and the radio news. Yet in place of clarity and comprehension, in every one of these examples confusion was sown and barriers to communication erected. Such **disorders in discourse** result from gaps between distinct and insufficiently coincident cognitive worlds: the gulfs that separate insiders from outsiders, members of institutions from clients of those institutions, and elites from the normal citizen uninitiated in the arcana of bureaucratic language and life. They are traceable not only to the use of unfamiliar professional or technical jargon, but also to the immanent structure of the discourses themselves. Thus, for example, insufficient semantic knowledge prevents listeners from updating the information they possess through radio news bulletins. In clinical conversations between doctors and patients the technical terminology doctors employ in making diagnoses and prescribing remedies is often impenetrable and intimidating to patients, reinforcing previously existing power relations. Such factors serve merely to intensify the exposed situation which patients experience in outpatient clinics – on the one hand healthy experts, on the other sick and dependent lay persons. The result is a so-called 'frame conflict': worlds of knowledge and interests collide with one another, and those who possess linguistic as well as institutional power invariably prevail. The problem is similar in everyday social interaction with public servants or official documents. Lay persons have little chance when faced with arcane legal regulations. Ignorance of the law, it seems, is no excuse, though it may be worthwhile to consider why, since for many citizens vitally important information remains structurally inaccessible.

Furthermore, members of an institution (the insiders) often do not understand each other. In a recent study where 34 managers observed their own interactions with other employees over a two-week period, the results show that only 12% of conversations were actually understood as intended and:

> ... that 75% of the reported interactions were registered by only one of the participants. Of the 25% of personal contacts, which both sides could still remember a few hours after they had occurred, 53% had not been understood by the recipient in the sense intended by the transmitter. Of the total of reported interactions, therefore, only 12% 'arrived', in the sense that both sides agreed both as to the occurrence and as to the meaning of the communication. (Archibald 1976: 200)

In this book I would like to present, with illustrative examples, an approach I have developed over several years' research (starting out with the analysis of courtroom interaction in the 70s and ending with the research of meetings in schools in the 90s) and which I have termed **discourse sociolinguistics**. Discourse sociolinguistics, as I understand it, is a sociolinguistics which not only is explicitly dedicated to the study of the text in context, but also accords both factors equal importance. It is an approach capable of identifying and describing the underlying mechanisms that contribute to those disorders in discourse which are embedded in a particular context – whether they be in the structure and function of the media, or in institutions such as a hospital or a school – and inevitably affect communication. Thus, the research in this book focuses, on the one hand, on discourses within institutions (between insiders and clients or between insiders), on the other hand on the impact of institutional products on lay persons in everyday life (news). In both cases, we diagnose disorders: misunderstanding and conflicts while communicating with each other; and misunderstanding and non-understanding while reading or listening to vital information which is produced by social elites (politicians, journalists, teachers) under the explicit assumption that this information should be accessible to everyone. The methodologies used are consequentially different in these two domains (see 1.4.2 below). The ethnographic approach predominates in the analysis of discourses within the institutions (inside-perspective). The approach from 'outside' through tests and interviews is necessary in the second case, complemented through observation from within, but without serious and systematic research into the text production (of news) (see Benke 1994, Hardt-Mautner 1992). Thus, this book also covers both sides of communication: discourse production (authentic discourses) (Chapter 2, 3, 5) and comprehension of discourses (Chapter 4) in a more experimental setting.

Discourse sociolinguistics, like critical linguistics (see 1.3.2 below), aims at de-mystifying the disorders mentioned above in the two domains of discourse, in actual language use in institutions and in the intersection of institution and everyday life. In both cases, we will also pose the question of possible changes (see 1.5.1., 1.5.2., 1.5.3 below): who benefits from reformulations, do different modes of discourse produce more understanding and fewer disorders? Or, to put in bluntly, are power structures only mystified in a more skilful way?

1.1.2. Dimensions of sociolinguistics

The first major steps in mapping the territory of sociolinguistics were taken in the 1960s. The most significant of these were Basil Bernstein's notion of 'speech barriers', William Labov's conception of 'difference', Roger Brown and Albert Gilman's idea of 'power and solidarity', and Dell Hymes' concept of 'communicative competence' (see Dittmar 1973, Hymes 1964, Leodolter 1975a). Since that time the theories informing sociolinguistic methods as well as the methods themselves have undergone significant change. Early sociolinguistic research in the USA, for example, seldom dealt with oral discourse, but restricted itself to the smallest linguistic units (socio-phonology). The context that was integrated into such analyses consisted of a few extralinguistic variables such as the social class, ethnicity and culture of the partners in the interaction.

Basil Bernstein (1970), whose background was in education studies, focused on the written essays of schoolchildren in Great Britain. He developed a theory which drew together linguistic competences, social class and socialization processes to explain significant differences in the language behaviour of middle-class and working-class children. His linguistic indicators were shown to be invalid, and he was subjected to furious attack over his 'deficit hypothesis'. Bernstein claimed that working-class children used a restricted code and had to be taught to compensate for their shortcomings. William Labov (1966, 1969), on the other hand, was mainly interested in factors that influence language change (Wodak/ Benke 1994). In his studies of Black English, Labov was able to prove that black children were not restricted in the Bernsteinian sense. Quite the contrary: they spoke their language as adequately as white children did their own. Both languages were adequate, simply different. Neither is seen to be worth more than the other. But Labov's approach lacks the social structural aspect, as he did not include societal values and norms in his considerations. He did not even sufficiently recognize that though black and white children have their own languages, standard English still claims far greater prestige.

Dell Hymes was influenced by ethnographic research. For him, language behaviour is clearly embedded in social contexts, and situational, structural and cultural factors determine communication. The term 'communicative competence' implies a sociolinguistic framework. 'Competence' is not viewed only as the property of a 'native speaker', as it is defined in the Chomskyan approach, but as fundamentally constituted in communication. Finally, Roger Brown and Albert Gilman (1968) made a study of the use of pronouns in address and developed their model of 'power and solidarity'. Forms of address depend on the power relationship between interactants, but also on the degree of formality or intimacy. This concept has been revived recently by Deborah Tannen (1990) in her study of gender-specific language behaviour. My own work on the language behaviour of defendants at court (Leodolter 1975a) bears the strong influence of all these approaches. It was one of the first sociolinguistic studies of institutional behaviour to focus on power and social class, using text-linguistic and phonological variables. The general framework of the present book, which I would like to summarize here, is grounded in the methodology of that first study, although twenty years of research have inevitably led to many new distinctions and elaborations, as will become clear in the chapters that follow. Thus chronological development also accounts for different modes of analysis within this book, starting out with a text linguistics as established in the 80s and ending with a complex discourse analysis which incorporates many new insights and results.

In more recent scholarship, the optic of sociolinguistics has been considerably expanded: oral communication has become a crucial object of sociolinguistic investigation, and an exclusive interest in phonological analysis and linguistic variation has given way to research at the level of the linguistic text, while the integration of new and different variables (such as gender) has considerably enhanced the methodological sophistication of sociolinguistics. In addition, concepts whose origins lay in the related disciplines of sociology, social psychology, depth psychology and history have acquired an essential heuristic function in the analysis of context in sociolinguistics. Jürgen Habermas' 'Lebenswelt' (world of life, i.e. qualitative research, 1981)[1] approach and Pierre Bourdieu's 'theory of symbolic capital' (1987) are perhaps the two most significant of such sociolinguistic borrowings in Europe.

Two major developments have thus characterized the change in sociolinguistic research over the last ten years. The first is the transition from the linguistic unit of the sentence or the phoneme to the 'text in context', that is to say, to discourse and the ensuing methodological convergence of the fields of discourse analysis and sociolinguistics. The second is the heightened attention given to the analysis of the context itself. This, in turn, has led to increasingly systematic commitment to interdisciplinary research; emblematic of this is the relationship of sociolinguistics to discourse analysis. This qualitative turn in sociolinguistics was to be welcomed, for the quantification of discourse proved far more difficult than the quantification of phonological or syntactic units; moreover, in some cases, such quantification is actually impossible. At the same time, the analysis of context has assumed a priority equal to that of the text. The discourse sociolinguistic approach which this book employs is designed to provide answers to several theoretical and methodological questions: what exactly are 'disorders in discourse' and how can they be identified in a given context? How are those in power able linguistically to predominate and thereby continually reproduce power relations? Do those who are disadvantaged have any chance of successfully asserting themselves? Which related disciplines, which sociological concepts, for example, are appropriate for delineating the macro-context, such as a hospital? To what extent does the specific discourse (institutional, media, etc.) determine the methods and tools of analysis? In other words, do oral texts enjoin analytical procedures different from those imposed by written texts? How narrowly or widely ought context to be defined in order to grasp the processes of understanding and non-understanding? How are the fundamental discourse units to be defined: how many conversation sequences are necessary, which discourse elements are to be chosen in a given context and why?

This book also addresses more 'praxis'-oriented (politically oriented) concerns: is it possible today to realize the emancipatory claims of sociolinguistics, i.e. can sociolinguistics help remedy the inequalities it identifies? Is it possible to use the results of such sociolinguistic studies to develop proposals that will help alter the linguistic behaviour of people in these institutions? In fact, all of the above questions may be seen to address one general problem, namely, that of what might be called 'negotiation and construction of understanding', or, more specifically, why there are so many disorders and such little understanding. It is here, in fact, that sociology and linguistics, and sociolinguistics and discourse theory, intersect. On the one hand, linguistic approaches are able to describe explicitly how conversations are structured, or how communication problems are constituted at the micro-level of the text itself. The typical patterns that can be identified relate to context, the speaker's gender, status or class, ethnicity, etc. On the other hand, quite different, sociological theories (e.g. the systems theory approach of Talcot Parsons or the 'critical theory' of Jürgen Habermas) describe the macro-structural conditions which promote or hinder social communication at the levels of the institution and society. The discourse sociolinguistics I wish to elucidate attempts to integrate these levels of analysis by correlating context and discourse, so as to explain why communicative behaviour varies according to the specific structural conditions in which it takes place. Through an analysis of micro-discourses it is possible to indicate the extent to which participants in interactions approach or retreat from mutually comprehensible communication.

The empirical data used to establish and illustrate the aspects of discourse sociolinguistics described above are taken from studies I have carried out over the past twenty years. Among the materials involved are conversations recorded in schools and in a hospital outpatient clinic, which detail interactions between teachers, head-teachers and pupils in elementary schools, and between doctors and patients in the clinic. For example, the detailed analysis of the daily routines of the outpatient clinic – seven morning shifts were recorded and subsequently transcribed – yielded a number of generalizations about frame conflicts in this context (Chapter 2). Similarly extensive data were collected in a qualitative study on understanding and comprehension in public discourse, namely, on the comprehension of radio new bulletins. The range of comprehension tests and in-depth interviews with test subjects made it possible to pinpoint those characteristics of discourse which restrict or disable understanding (Chapter 4). Moreover, the results obtained in these latter studies with texts reformulated to facilitate comprehension suggest that understanding can be technically improved, but only to a limited extent: experience and background knowledge are also essential to the success of efforts to enhance the process of comprehension.

Before I present the case studies, I would like to provide the reader with some general orientation: Firstly, definitions of key elements in the institutional discourse will be discussed (see 1.2 below). All the data were collected in organizations[2] in Vienna over the last twenty years, by the author herself, or together with fellow researchers. In this section, I will focus on both terms, on 'institution' and on 'discourse'. Secondly, in relation to Foucault (1993), though in contrast to him, I will discuss the issue of 'orders' and 'disorders' in institutional discourse (see 1.5 below). Thirdly, this introductory chapter will provide the reader with the general methodology applied in the empirical research, through the paradigm of **discourse sociolinguistics** (see 1.4 below). The notion of context is essential in this approach. Lastly, we will pose the question as to what a **critical discourse sociolinguistic analysis** of institutional discourse is seeking to achieve (see 1.5.3 below). Then, what are its results, what are their consequences? In considering these questions, I would like to contrast two theoretical concepts, the concept of the 'ideal speech situation' developed by Habermas (1969, 1970a, b,) and the genealogical poststructuralist concept of 'discourse' elaborated by Foucault (1993) (see 1.5.1, 1.5.2 below). I would like to state at the outset that I will not take sides with either of these two approaches; following Fairclough (1992) and Giddens (1988), I shall elaborate a number of points of criticism and mention several relevant issues that have to be integrated into any epistemological framework for discourse sociolinguistics and applied linguistics.[3]

1.2 Institutional discourse

'Communication theorists pay little attention to organizations and organizational theorists little attention to communication' (Roberts *et al.* 1977: 501). This situation is now slowly changing in the social sciences. Both aspects have become more considered, more fully integrated into different theoretical approaches, using varying methods of analysing discourse.[4] Discourse is seen as constitutive of institutions. Thus, Deetz (1982: 135) remarks that

> of all institutional forms, language has a special position. All other institutional forms may be translated into language ... Further, every perception is dependent on the conceptual apparatus which makes it possible and meaningful, as this conceptual apparatus is inscribed in language. Talk and writing are thus much more than the means of expression of individual meanings; they connect each perception to a larger orientation and system of meaning. The conceptual distinctions in an organization are inscribed in the systems of speaking and writing. Speaking and writing are thus epistemic.

Organizing is therefore continuously created and re-created in the act of communication between organizational members. Similarly, though from the perspective of conversational analysis, Drew/ Heritage (1992: 3) here characterize the relevance of the relationship between institutions and communication:

> Talk in interaction is the principal means through which lay persons pursue various practical goals and the central medium through which the daily working activities of many professionals and organizational representatives are conducted. We will use the term 'institutional interaction' to refer to talk of this kind.

Before we try to grasp the relationship between discourse and institutions in a more detailed way, we would like to present two definitions of institution which we consider important, and which stress different aspects and are thus complementary. Mumby (1988: 3) stresses the notion of 'organizational cultures':

> This approach conceptualizes organizations as cultures in order to examine the ways in which organization members engage in the creation of organizational reality. Such research generally takes organizational symbolism – myths, stories, legends, jokes, rites, logos – as the most clearly visible articulation of organizational reality.

Mumby argues further, that most cultural approaches to organization start with the concepts of 'shared meaning' and 'sense-making'. He criticizes the neglect of the concept of power, the fact that – as I also illustrate in my case studies – meanings are not shared inside the institution. Quite the contrary: the everyday life of institutions is characterized by conflicts, by disorders in discourse, by contradictions which are mystified through myths and other symbols of the institution (see Chapter 2; Archibald 1976).

For Mumby, power is a structural phenomenon, a product of, and a process by which, the members of an organization engage in organizing activity. Organizational power is constituted and reproduced through the structure of organizational symbolism. Power manifests itself in hierarchies, in access to specific discourses and information and, most particularly, in the establishment of symbols. Which myths are considered relevant, or which ideologies, norms and values are posited, relates directly to the groups in power and their interests. A good example of the symbolic constitution of organizational hierarchy is to be found in meetings (see Chapter 3):

> meetings are perceived as a necessary and pervasive characteristic of organizational life – they are events that people are required to engage in if decisions are to be made and goals to be accomplished. While this is the ostensible rationale for meetings, they also function as one of the most important and visible sites of organizational power, and of the reification of organizational hierarchy. (Mumby 1988: 68)

The concept of institutions viewed as cultures with an emphasis on discourse and power lends itself well to the analysis in the following chapters. The specific methodology used in our empirical investigations (see 2.3.1 below; the inside-perspective) suggests clearly that institutions have their own 'life', their own rules, insider jokes and stories which are narrated over and over again and serve to strengthen the status quo (e.g. the archetypical story of how people 'make' it). By observing an institution from the inside, by participating in meetings and other rituals or by following the insiders through their everyday life at work, the mixture and interwovenness of all these many discourses become apparent (see, for example, 5.2 below).

As mentioned above, institutions have their own value systems, which are crystallized in the form of particular ideologies. However, it is important to distinguish between the explicit demands and expectations of an official institutional ideology, and the implicit rules underlying everyday behaviour. These two sets of norms often lead to contradictions: for example, van Dijk (1993b) discusses a study of managers in large companies, who claimed in interviews that foreigners had equal chances of employment and that they overtly supported 'affirmative' action, whereas in reality foreigners were at the time actively discriminated against in those companies. Such contradictions are disguised by what Barthes (1974) calls 'myths', and in this way they become legitimized. Myths in this sense of the word are secondary semiotic systems, which both insiders and outsiders are supposed to believe and which mystify reality. A second reality is thus constructed and naturalized. A striking example of this in medical institutions is the great knowledge that doctors are assumed to possess and their alleged infallibility: 'Götter in weiss' (gods in white) is a common expression in Austrian German (see 2.6 for a description of other important myths in hospitals).

Giddens (1989: 275ff) provides us with a more functional

definition of institutions and organizations: 'an organization is a large association of people run on impersonal lines, set up to achieve specific goals. Most social systems in the traditional world developed over lengthy periods of time as a result of custom and habit' (1989: 276). Moreover, Giddens stresses the fact that organizations are housed in specific buildings or physical settings which help realize these aims. Thus, when studying organizations, one should not neglect the 'objective' setting, the architecture, as this manifests and also constitutes the reality of the system. We shall return to this question when discussing the construction and analysis of the context of institutional discourse (see 1.4.1 below).

Another important factor mentioned by Giddens is the dynamics of organizations: they develop over time, and they change. This historical dimension has to be included when investigating specific discourses. Discourses are marked by **intertextuality**, and are always related to other discourses, synchronically and diachronically (Fairclough/Wodak 1996). For example, the specificities of medical interaction can only be understood against the background of the development of medical institutions per se (see Foucault 1979, Renkeema 1993: 44ff): rules are not immutable and the communicative patterns that characterize them differ with changed historical circumstance. Also, traditional elements are often well preserved but lose their original function and thereby become rituals (ritual formulations in legal language; see Danet 1984, Pfeiffer/Strouhal/Wodak 1987, Gibbons 1994).

Giddens' theory of structuration (Giddens 1979, 1981, 1982) also explicitly rejects the concept of the social actor as wholly subject to the structures of power and domination embodied in the organization, and argues instead that organizational practices have a potentially transformative capacity. He argues further that the capacity for both domination and emancipation is integrated in the everyday practices of organizational life. This opinion contrasts strongly with other theories of institutions (see Foucault 1993, Fairclough 1992, and 1.5.1 below). The 'dialectic of control', as Giddens calls it, focuses on the ability of the social actor, as agent, to engage in choice, however restrictive the conditions may be. Thus, 'The dialectic of control is implied ... in the logical connection between agency and power. An agent who has no opinions whatsoever is no longer an agent' (Giddens 1981: 63). Organizations are not simply viewed as constraints on action, but also function in an enabling capacity, allowing members of the organization to reach goals, develop value systems, etc. Agency and structure are interdependent (see also Mumby 1988: 51ff).

The case studies presented in this book integrate both approaches: I agree that institutional reality is produced and reproduced through discourse, on the one hand; on the other hand, I would like to stress the dialectic between 'objective' reality (such as buildings) and the inside life of the organization. The discourse sociolinguistic approach allows us to differentiate the 'culture' concept, to analyse the interaction at the micro-level and thus make the complexity of meanings, norms and values transparent. There exists not *one* discourse in the institution, but a whole set of interwoven, conflicting discourses which construct and establish multiple relationships. Thus, I would like to point to the great importance of analysing power relationships in institutional discourse. I do not view agents as completely powerless and subjected to action by elites. This has serious implications for our methodology and also for our practical work, for example in our attempts to change institutions via changes of discourse (see 1.5.3 below).

1.3 Disorders of discourse within organizations

1.3.1 How do we define 'discourse'?

The term 'discourse'[5] integrates a range of meanings in its everyday and philosophical uses, which sometimes seem to contradict or exclude one another. Fairclough (1992: 3ff) points to several ways in which the concept is used, most especially how they arise in modern discourse analysis: 'samples of spoken dialogue, in contrast with written texts'; 'spoken and written language'; 'situational context of language use'; 'interaction between reader/writer and text'; 'notion of genre' (for example, newspaper discourse). These various meanings are often used in an unreflecting way. Frequently it is unclear whether a short text sequence is meant or a whole variety of text, or whether a very abstract phenomenon is to be understood under this heading.[6] Consequently in our own exposition we shall try to clearly define – and distinguish between – the concepts of discourse, text and discourse analysis.

It is not possible in this section to provide an overview of all developments in discourse analysis or all the different notions of 'discourse' established in divergent paradigms (see van Dijk 1985: 4ff, 1990; Schiffrin 1993: 21ff; Renkeema 1993; Vass 1992: 9). Instead, I would like to focus only on definitions that are important for the analysis presented in this book. I will start out by differentiating between 'text' and 'discourse'. Then, I shall offer my own approach to the concept of 'discourse' which has developed and changed over many years of studying institutions from a discourse sociolinguistic point of view. I shall mention the main intellectual currents that influenced my own theoretical and methodological development and led to a concept of discourse which finally shares elements but is not identical with the approaches of Teun van Dijk (1990: 163ff, 1993a) and Norman Fairclough (Fairclough 1992: 62ff; Fairclough/Wodak 1996) (see 1.3.2 below).

1.3.1.1 Discourse and text

Gisela Brünner and Gabriele Graefen (1993b: 2) characterize the main differences between 'text' and 'discourse' in the following way:

> By *discourse* are to be understood units and forms of speech, of interaction, which can be part of everyday linguistic behaviour, but which can equally appear in an institutional sphere. Orality, admittedly, is not a feature which holds true for *all* forms of discursive behaviour ... but is very much the typical case. Regarded systematically, discourse requires the co-presence of speaker and listener ('face-to-face interaction'); this can, however, be reduced to a temporal co-presence (on the telephone). [my translation]

On the other hand, they also define discourse as the totality of interactions in a certain domain (medical discourse, for example), which appears similiar to the definition offered by Foucault (see 1.5.1 below). 'Text', however, has different roots, in philology and literature:

> In the context of a theory of linguistic behaviour, it is an essential determination of the text, that the linguistic behaviour, which is made material in the text, is detached from the overall common speech situation just as is the receptive behaviour of the reader – the common ground being understood in a systematic, not a historical sense. In a text, speech behaviour assumes the quality of knowledge, which is in the service of transmission and is stored for later use; ...

the written form, which is constitutive for the everyday use of the term, and today is frequently regarded as almost synonymous with 'text', is therefore not a necessary feature of a text. [my translation]

Text does not have to be written, according to Brünner/Graefen (1993b), discourse does not have to be oral. The main difference lies in the function of 'handing down [Überlieferung]' and in the simultaneous existence (or absence) of a situational context. Discourse may thus be defined as 'text in context' (van Dijk 1990: 164) on the one hand; as a 'set of texts' on the other (Dressler/Merlini-Barbaresi 1994: 6ff). In this book, I shall use 'discourse' with both these meanings.[7] Below, I present the most recent definition of 'discourse' in critical discourse analysis, which brings together all these aspects.

Van Dijk (1990: 164) points to an additional decisive aspect, which is that discourse should also be understood as action: 'I understand "discourse" ... both as a specific form of language use, and as a specific form of social interaction, interpreted as a complete communicative event in a social situation'. The behavioural aspect is very important to my definition. In my earlier work I made use of Ludwig Wittgenstein's concepts of 'language game' and 'form of life', as well as of Jürgen Habermas' concept of 'ordinary language' (see 1.3.1.2 below; Leodolter 1975a: 27); indeed all three are of crucial importance to the development of speech act theory, which, however, I do not wish to deal with in detail here (see 1.5.2; Schiffrin 1993: 49; Wodak 1986a: 229), since I refer to written and oral discourses and not to speech acts at the level of the sentence/phrase.

The self-contained communicative act is the centre of interest. This points to a fundamentally more difficult and complex question, which is the extent to which a unit of discourse may be defined as self-contained at all. We shall return to that question again in our methodological remarks (1.4.1.). At this point, it only needs to be noted that, in terms of the range of the concept, *in principle* – because of intertextuality – there is no objective beginning and no clearly defined end, because every discourse is related to many others and can only be understood on the basis of others. The limitations of the research area therefore depend on a subjective decision by the researcher, and on the formulation of the questions guiding the research (Kress 1993).

I would like, above all, to emphasize the behavioural aspect even more strongly and I therefore suggest the following definition of discourse provided by critical discourse analysis (CDA) before proceeding further (Fairclough 1992: 62; Fairclough/Wodak 1996):

> *Critical discourse analysis sees discourse – the use of language in speech and writing – as a form of 'social practice'.* Describing discourse as social practice implies a dialectical relationship between a particular discursive event and the situation, institution and social structure that frame it: the discursive event is shaped by them, but it also shapes them. That is, discourse is socially constituted, as well as socially conditioned – it constitutes situations, objects of knowledge, and the social identities of and relationships between people and groups of people. It is constitutive both in the sense that it helps sustain and reproduce the social status quo, and in the sense that it contributes to transforming it. [my emphasis]

That provides a direct link to our discussion of organizations and institutions, in which we emphasized the reality-constituting element of discourse.[8] In addition it becomes evident that questions of power and ideology are connected with discourse:

> Since discourse is so socially consequential, it gives rise to important issues of power. Discursive practices may have major ideological effects – that is, they can help produce and reproduce unequal power relations ... through the ways in which they represent things and position people. (Fairclough/Wodak 1996)

Discourse sociolinguistics thus practises critical discourse analysis and adheres to certain principles of CDA, as I will demonstrate below (1.3.2). Genuinely sociolinguistic approaches such as are extensively enumerated and deployed in the case studies, are consequently investigated by way of discourses which originate in organizations and are all connected with questions of power and ideology. The distortion of discourse (in Habermas' sense, see 1.5.2) leads to 'disorders of discourse' in actually occurring everyday interaction. Understanding is the exception, misunderstanding and conflict are the rule. The distortions, however, are of a quite systematic nature and correspond to more abstract orders of discourse, as described by Foucault (cf. 1.5.1). In contrast to Foucault, however, I am dealing with empirical discourses and I will demonstrate that even the obvious disorders of discourse are ultimately systematic and connected to social structure. There is therefore also an order in disorder. Critical discourse analysis is an instrument whose purpose is precisely to expose veiled power structures: 'CDA aims to make more visible these opaque aspects of discourse' (Fairclough/Wodak 1996).

1.3.1.2 Discourse as action

The idea of regarding language as expression, and a part of social forms of life in terms of a rule-bound game, derives from analytical philosophy, beginning with Ludwig Wittgenstein. According to this approach, speech follows specific rules – just like a game.

> Let us imagine a language for which the description given by Augustine is right. The language is meant to serve for communication between a builder A and an assistant B. A is building with building-stones: there are blocks, pillars, slabs and beams. B has to pass the stones, and that in the order which A needs them. For this purpose they use a language consisting of the words 'block', 'pillar', 'slab', 'beam'. A calls them out; B brings the stone which he has learnt to bring at such-and-such a call. Conceive this as a complete primitive language. (Wittgenstein 1967: ¶2)

And Wittgenstein continues (1967: ¶7): 'I will call these games "language-games" and will sometimes speak of a primitive language as a language-game ... I shall also call the whole, consisting of language and the actions into which it is woven, "the language-game".'

It becomes evident that language is very closely related to action, that speaking is action and that certain situations are thereby created. Speech is, therefore, an expression of action, as well as constitutive of it.

This leads us back to our reflections on institutions as cultures in which speech behaviour also possesses a reality-constituting function (see 1.2 above). Simultaneously it would also be possible to advance this Wittgensteinian concept as a foundation for the concept of discourse outlined above, in which a dialectic between discourse and reality is noted.[9] We therefore regard 'speech' not as a purely intellectual, cognitive process, but more as a part of an action, a 'form of life'. Accordingly, discourse sociolinguistics investigates – in metatheoretical terms – socio-cultural forms of life.

Here the term 'language-game' is meant to bring into prominence the fact that the *speaking* of language is part of an activity, or of a form of life.

Review the multiplicity of language-games in the following examples, and in others:

Giving orders, and obeying them –
Describing the appearence of an object, or giving its measurements –
Constructing an object from a description (a drawing) –
Reporting an event –
Speculating about an event –
Forming and testing a hypothesis –
Making a joke; telling it –
Solving a problem in practical arithmetic –
Translating from one language into another –
Asking, thanking, cursing, greeting, praying.
(Wittgenstein 1967: ¶23)

This list is very reminiscent of an enumeration of performatives and speech acts (see 1.5.2 below). Speech acts, therefore, designate an action and simultaneously carry it out. Discourse sociolinguistics investigates, on the one hand, social conditions which affect such forms of life and influence social behaviour, and, on the other hand, expression in discourse, the link between discourse and behaviour in interactions, in situations.

To sum up, discourses are, therefore, multi-layered, verbal and non-verbal, they are rule-bound, the rules being either manifest or latent, they determine actions and also manifest them, they are embedded in forms of life (cultures), of which they are simultaneously co-constituent. Critical discourse analysis, which serves as a framework for discourse sociolinguistics, is in the process of developing its own methods and tools in order to analyse discourses, which are 'distorted' by power and ideology.

1.3.2 *Some principles of critical discourse analysis (CDA)* [10]

1 CDA addresses social problems: CDA is the analysis of linguistic and semiotic aspects of social processes and problems. The focus is not upon language or the use of language in and of themselves, but upon the linguistic character of social and cultural processes and structures. CDA is by its nature interdisciplinary, combining diverse disciplinary perspectives in its analysis, and being used to complement more

prevalent forms of social and cultural analysis. The main focus of the investigation in the case studies presented in this book is the nature of miscommunication, of non-understanding, of disorders of discourse. In all the empirical studies, I wish to find out what the power relations are like and to what kind of communication or non-communication they lead.

2   Power relations are discursive: CDA highlights the substantively linguistic and discursive nature of social relations of power in contemporary societies. This is partly a matter of how power relations are exercised and negotiated in discourse. It is fruitful to look at both 'power in discourse' and 'power over discourse' in these dynamic terms: both the exercise of power in the 'here and now' of specific discursive events, and the longer-term shaping of discursive practices and orders of discourse, are generally negotiated and contested processes. In my study on discourse in school meetings, I investigate access to discourse and information which is extremely restricted, usually to the school principal. In these meetings, hierarchies are reproduced through discourse (see Chapter 3).

3   Discourse constitutes society and culture: We can only make sense of the salience of discourse in contemporary social processes and power relations by recognizing that discourse constitutes society and culture, as well as being constituted by them. The relationship is dialectical, and every instance of language use makes its own contribution to reproducing or transforming culture and society, including power relations. The analysis of doctor–patient communication in an outpatient clinic illustrates how the structure of this organization is constantly created and reproduced through discourse (see Chapter 2).

4   Discourse does ideological work: Ideologies are particular ways of representing and constructing society which reproduce unequal relations of power, relations of domination and exploitation. Ideologies are often (though not necessarily) false or ungrounded constructions of society (e.g. gender ideologies which represent women as less emotionally stable than men). To determine whether a particular type of discursive event does ideological work, it is not enough to analyse texts – one also needs to consider how texts are interpreted and received and what social effects texts have. CDA, on the other hand, does

not claim that all discourse is ideological: 'It does not follow that because all practices are in ideology, or inscribed by ideology, all practices are nothing but ideology' (Hall 1985: 103). My study of news broadcasts and their possible reformulations, which were tested with a large sample group, illustrates how the process of comprehension is influenced by many attitudes, prejudices and ideologies. News texts themselves include many values and norms (see Chapter 4).

5   Discourse is historical: Discourse is not produced and cannot be understood without taking the context into consideration. This relates, on a metatheoretical level, to Wittgenstein's notions of 'language-game' and 'forms of life' (Wittgenstein 1967) (see 1.3.1.2 above); utterances are only meaningful if we consider their use in a specific situation, if we recognize their embedding in a certain culture and ideology, and most importantly, if we know what the discourse relates to in the past. Discourses are always connected to other discourses which were produced earlier, as well as those which are produced synchronically or subsequently ('the intertextuality of a text'). While analysing therapeutic discourse in group therapy, it could be made clear that specific sequences are only understandable against the background of many other factors: personal characteristics of the patients, their life histories, the dynamics in the group itself etc. (see Chapter 5)

6   The link between text and society, between the micro and the macro, is mediated: We assume a mode of mediation between the actual, realized text and the wider social practices in which the piece of text is embedded. We can also formulate this in a different way: how do speakers realize their intentions, beliefs and ideologies in discourse, and how do listeners interpret a spoken text, given their own beliefs, attitudes, knowledge and ideologies? The socio-psychological model of text comprehension suggests a socio-cognitive approach to finding a link between text and society (see Chapter 4).

7   Discourse analysis is interpretive and explanatory: Critical reading implies a systematic methodology and a thorough investigation of context (see 1.4.2 below). This might narrow down the range of possible readings. The heterogeneity and vagueness of the text condenses contradictions which only become apparent through careful analysis. The text is thus

deconstructed and embedded in its social conditions, is linked to ideologies and power relationships. This marks the point where critical readings differ from those that are uncritical. Interpretations are never finished and authoritative, they are dynamic and open, open to new contexts and new information. The three-level model for the analysis of therapeutic discourse provides us with an example for a systematic methodology which makes interpretations of the discourse possible (see Chapter 5).

8   Discourse is a form of social action: CDA is a socially committed scientific paradigm. CDA is not less 'scientific' than other linguistic approaches: critical linguists make their interests explicit, unlike other scholars in many other disciplines. Critical linguists have had some success in changing discourse and power patterns in organizations. For example, while analysing doctor–patient communication, it became apparent that over and above their expert knowledge, doctors use many other strategies to dominate their clients (see Chapter 2). The critical analysis of such patterns led to the establishment of guidelines for different behaviour patterns which are now taught in seminars for doctors. The same is true for other institutions, for bureaucracies, legal institutions and schools, as well as for the media (see Chapters 3, 4).

1.4 Methodological considerations: inside versus outside perspective

1.4.1 Context

This study is based on research over the past twenty years. Much has changed since my first study, on the language behaviour of defendants at court (Leodolter 1975a, Wodak 1980, 1984, 1985). For example, in the 1970s, discourse analysis in the present sense of the term did not even exist. Text linguistics was slowly being developed (see Beaugrande/Dressler 1981, Vass 1992), and linguistic analysis had only just begun to transcend the level of the sentence. On the other hand, sociolinguistics at that time focused primarily on phonological units and quantitative analyses of a correlative nature (Wodak/Benke 1994). Pragmatics and then slowly the emerging paradigm of discourse analysis, on the other hand, led to qualitative analyses of small text sequences, often without reference to the macro-context.[11] The approach which I am suggesting – discourse sociolinguistics – tries to combine several methods of a qualitative and quantitative nature while analysing discourse from a sociolinguistic point of view. Also, I believe, context should be integrated in a more holistic manner than previously.

Context was traditionally defined through the inclusion of static sociological variables, such as class, gender, ethnicity and age. Situational contexts or cognitive and emotional factors regarding the speakers and audience were not included. In my study of therapeutic discourse (1986a), I had used participant observation to try to understand the life and culture of the institution. The data were not restricted to specific discourse sequences, but included all verbal and non-verbal actions in the therapeutic group. As much additional information as possible was gathered and analysed with respect to its influence on the behaviour of the patients and therapists (see Chapter 5). Thus, context was defined far more broadly. We may perhaps visualize this methodology in the form of concentric circles. The smallest circle is the discourse unit itself and the micro-analysis of the text. The next circle consists of the speakers and audience, of the interactants with their various personality features, biographies and social roles. The next context level involves the 'objective setting', the location in time and space, the description of the situation. Then, the next circle signifies the institution in which the event takes place. And we could naturally expand to the society in which this institution is integrated, its function in society and its history. At all points, intertextuality is important; because of the specific problem under investigation, we should include other information which relates to our problem, such as other discourses of the same speakers, other events in the same institution, etc.[12] The integration of all these context levels would then lead to an analysis of discourse as social practice.

Cicourel distinguishes between two kinds of contexts, a broad and a local context. He argues that the broad context includes the institutionalized framing of activities, whereas emergent processes of talk create a narrower view of context in the sense of locally organized and negotiated interaction (Cicourel 1992: 295). Thus, Cicourel proposes a compromise between two positions, between the pure ethnographic approach and the conversational analysis

(CA) approach, which only considers the context created by the discourse itself (Drew/Heritage 1992: 16ff). CA relies *inter alia* on Gumperz' notion of 'contextualization cues': any aspect of linguistic behaviour – lexical, prosodic, phonological and syntactic choices, together with the use of particular codes, dialects or styles – may function as such, indicating those aspects of the context which are relevant in interpreting what a speaker means (Gumperz 1982: 162). There is a close affinity between the notion of contextualization cues and Goffman's concept of 'frame' (Goffman 1974, 1981). Frame focuses on the definition which participants give to their current social activity – to what is going on, what the situation is like, and to the roles that the interactants adopt within it. The subjective experience of the individuals in an interaction has to be taken into account while analysing discourse. Participants, Drew and Heritage claim, organize their conduct so as to display and realize its institutional character over its course, and they are doing so recurrently and pervasively (Drew/Heritage 1992: 20ff).

I would like to follow Cicourel's proposal to include both macro- (broad) and micro- (narrow, local) levels in the analysis. On the one hand, much necessary information is obtained through the ethnographic study; on the other hand, many markers and signals in the discourse itself manifest the speaker's perception and definition of context. Context is constructed and created through discourse, at the local level.[13] Lastly, we are confronted with a difficult problem: how do we know how much information will be necessary? I would like to quote Cicourel on this question:

> A nagging issue that undoubtedly remains for many readers is the familiar one that an infinite regress can occur whereby the observer presumably must describe 'everything' about a context. Such a demand is of course impossible to satisfy because no one could claim to have specified all of the local and larger sociocultural aspects of a context. Observers or analysts, like participants in speech events, must continually face practical circumstances that are an integral part of research of everyday living. (Cicourel 1992: 309)

Cicourel claims that what is most important is for observers to justify explicitly what has been included and what excluded as a result of theoretical goals, methodologies employed, and the consistency and convincingness of an argument or analysis.

1.4.2 Qualitative and quantitative methods

For decades already, there has been a dispute in the social sciences about the relevance of quantitative and qualitative methods (Dittmar 1983, Ehlich 1982, Wodak 1992, 500 ff). But do these two approaches really exclude each other? I believe not and would like to propose that the two methodologies complement each other. Both quantitative and qualitative research are necessary; comprehensive participant research and statistical generalizations are dependent on one another and only together can they provide an explicative mosaic of the object under investigation. I would like to name this approach the **multi-method approach**. Following these considerations, I have tried to apply to my case studies several methods that grasp different aspects of the institutions (see, e.g., Chapters 4 and 5). Interviews, questionnaires, tests, participant observation and micro-analysis of discourse sequences are needed for different phenomena and provide us with different results, all relating to the same macro-problem of power structures in organizations. We learn to understand and recognize certain processes in individuals through micro-research and case study. Statistical generalizations allow us to check whether the results yield typical patterns, and to relate them to social and cultural frameworks. In other words, statistical calculations provide descriptions, and allow correlations and dependencies to be established. Causes, motives and the dynamics of communicative behaviour are not covered by this.

In addition to the multi-method approach, we need to distinguish several levels of communicative behaviour as well as several dimensions of meanings: the social (macro) level, the subcultural (group) level and the level of the individual. Only this broad spectrum of meanings makes it possible to gain access to individual communicative behaviour. I would like to label this approach the **multi-level analysis** of discourse (see Chapter 5 for details). In every linguistic utterance, there are social and individual aspects. Every utterance is based on a multitude of motives, both conscious and subconscious, even of a conflicting nature. A thorough and subtle analysis of discourse should embrace all these meanings; the precision naturally depends on the amount of information on the context that is available.

1.5   Orders, disorders and ideal speech situation: what is the impact of discourse sociolinguistic research?

1.5.1   *Foucault*

The title of this book alludes to Foucault's inaugural lecture (Collège de France, 2 December 1970) (Foucault 1993). In this lecture, Foucault states his general presupposition in relationship to discourse:[14]

> I make the assumption that the production of discourse is at once controlled, selected, organized and canalized in every society – and that this is done by way of certain procedures, whose task it is to subdue the powers and dangers of discourse, to evade its heavy and threatening materiality. (Foucault 1993: 10–11)

In the course of his lecture, Foucault identifies the three most important procedures of exclusion: prohibition; the contrast between rationality and madness; and the contrast between right and wrong. Why is it necessary to pose constraints on the discourse?

Foucault arrives at a code of the 'discursive', which first of all defines itself as the endless texture of language in the world, a view which is typical of French structuralism of the 1950s and 60s in all its aspects. There exists no 'prelinguistic being in the world' for the subject, nor an original experience or an initial harmony with the world, which would make it possible (for the subject) to speak about it a priori and to deduce the basis of the sayable from the visible. In the beginning is an indefinite anonymous murmuring, in which the rankings and positions for the possible subjects are designated. Everything has the character of a sign, each sign refers to another in an unending series. Discourse possesses an autonomy constructed in such a way, which 'has something unique, threatening, even perhaps pernicious about it'.

He goes on to say, in his inaugural lecture, that our society respects discourse, that there is a logophilia, which is spreading. Underneath this logophilia, however, there is fear:

> It appears that the prohibitions, checks, threshholds and boundaries have the task of at least partly curbing the rampant growth of discourse, of divesting its richness of its greatest dangers and of organising its disorder [sic!], so that the least controllable is avoided;

it also looks as if an attempt had even been made to obliterate the traces of its inroads into thought and language. In our society, even if a different song is sung, there is undoubtedly a profound logophobia, a mute fear of those events . . . of the great unceasing murmur of discourse. (Foucault 1993: 33)

According to Foucault, certain strategies must regulate this disorder: principles of exclusion and reduction, in which 'the most visible and familiar [procedure] is the prohibition' (1993: 11). Important conventions of discourse are established by prohibition, for example that it is not possible to speak about everything on every occasion and that everyone cannot speak about everything. Since, because of the primary disorder and violence of discourse, we can never know exactly what the other person means, a perspective of power is imposed on discourse, so that again various mechanisms take effect. Every discursive setting is limited by rules and conventions, whereby many other possibilities are excluded (reduction and exclusion). But power is not seen solely as a form of oppression, it is also productively transformed. Only a setting with conventions and rules within a discursive space produces knowledge and makes possible, by way of exclusion and prohibition, a communicative framework, which can altogether be defined as functional. So, for example, the power of the doctor in a precisely defined setting, such as a clinic, permits the diagnosis of illness in the patient (see Chapter 2).

Foucault calls the second group of procedures internal procedures. In this case discourses exercise control themselves, with 'procedures, which operate as principles of classification, arrangement, distribution. This time it is a question of curbing another dimension of discourse: that of the event and of chance' (Foucault 1993: 17). Discourse collections (texts, rituals, formulae) are commented on and new discourses produced. Commentaries repeat the text, in a different form, but nothing is any longer left to chance.

The third group of procedures exercise control over the speaking individuals, 'in order to prevent anybody having access to discourses: reduction this time of the speaking subjects' (1993: 25). Only someone who possesses the necessary educational capital is allowed to lay claim to certain discourses. Here Foucault is reminiscent of Bourdieu, for whom various capitals constitute the value of an individual on a market. All the procedures mentioned can easily be related to a discourse sociolinguistic approach, although on a rather abstract level, since Foucault only rarely analyses empirical texts. Power is integral to discourse. Communication is never free of power, because otherwise there would be disorder (cf. also Fairclough 1992: 56).

In his genealogical phase, Foucault also deals with changes in discourses (and institutions). Power relationships admittedly change, but power continues to exist, always wearing new masks (Habermas 1985: 297–8). Power constantly clothes itself anew, more subtly, so Foucault thinks, power always being very closely linked to knowledge:

> On the one hand, the techniques of power are developed on the basis of knowledge which is generated, for example, in the social sciences; on the other hand, the techniques are very much concerned with exercising power in the process of gathering knowledge. Foucault coins the term 'bio-power' to refer to this modern form of power, which has emerged since the seventeenth century. (Fairclough 1992: 50)

The two most important techniques which Foucault distinguishes are 'discipline' and 'confession' (Foucault 1981). Discipline is intended to produce conforming people, 'docile bodies'. Discipline isolates the individual from the masses and subjects him or her to procedures of normalization. Thus the modern individual comes into being. Examination, the most important technique of discipline, gives rise to 'power relations that make it possible to extract and constitute knowledge' (Foucault 1979: 185). Visible power, for example, became invisible (in the course of the transition from feudal lord to abstract state power). Further, examination also leads to the registration and documentation of persons, whereby on the one hand descriptions become possible, while on the other hand statistics and generalizations do as well. In addition, documentation makes possible the preparation of 'cases', e.g. in medicine, where the human being is degraded to a case. Discipline also serves to objectify human beings.

Confession on the other hand serves to subjectify human beings. One talks about oneself and one's own needs, under the illusion that one is thereby liberating oneself. In reality, however, argues Foucault, one only submits even more to a power, an authority, to whom one is confessing. And this authority relationship is constitutive: 'one does not confess without the presence of a partner who is not simply the interlocutor but the authority who requires the confession, prescribes and appreciates it, and intervenes in order to judge, forgive, console and reconcile' (Fairclough 1992: 53). Through confession one gains the impression that one is changing oneself, but in fact one is conforming even further. Consultations, therapies and interview techniques are all forms of confession. Once again concrete text analyses are absent in Foucault. Fairclough (1992: 55) takes up Foucault's theoretical reflections to support his own arguments on the 'technologization and marketization' of discourse. According to him, other discursive practices, from advertising and counselling, for example, influence many institutional spheres, altering and concealing traditional discourses and ultimately mystifying power relationships.

When we ask what changes in the rules and conventions of discourse really mean, and this question is, of course, very important to applied linguistics, then Foucault's answer is that some discourses become superficially more pleasant, less oppressive, but that in fact power continues to exist – and even better hidden than before. Changed techniques of communication, e.g. between doctors and patients, are not, therefore, emancipatory, but even more subtle in the exercise of power. Reviewing the results of my empirical studies, this is certainly true in some cases, but certainly not in all. If, for example, the doctors become more polite, then the patients accepts their 'orders' more readily, but they also find it easier to dare to ask questions and perhaps even to discuss problems. This presents new possibilities for the patients, though only – as my case studies demonstrate – up to a certain point, at which the doctors feel their own power threatened (cf. Chapter 2). Does this change in the pattern of discourse only mean conformity, or does it also imply a certain degree of liberation? I believe that the patients sound out their chances and are, as a result, ultimately better informed, are no longer quite so helpless when confronted by the institution. Foucault on the other hand ultimately denies the subject the possibility of active intervention; the individuals always remain helpless. I shall come back to that below, once I have examined more closely a second theory on the transformation of discourses.

1.5.2 Habermas

Mumby (1988: 23ff) points to four key domains discussed by Habermas (1969, 1970a, b, 1975, 1979):

- Knowledge does not exist as an independent entity, but is derived from knowledge-constituting interests. These interests (technical, practical and emancipatory) influence everyday knowledge and the knowledge produced by social enquiry.
- The theory of interests is fundamental for a critique of ideology and domination. The focus, for example, of capitalist societies on technical-rational knowledge results in a preference for technical interests and a cult of 'the expert'.
- The critique of ideology and domination is elaborated by Habermas through his theory of 'communicative competence', which expresses emancipatory interest. Self-reflection is the basic process through which emancipation can be achieved, psychoanalysis is proposed as a model for such a process (see Wodak 1986a: 19ff). Underlying this theory is the utopia of an ideal speech situation.
- The critique of ideology which Habermas also refers to as 'systematically distorted communication' allows him to examine the process of legitimation in capitalist societies. He argues that generalizable interests have become subordinated to privatized needs of elites. Thus, a false consensus is produced through power and domination.

In this section I will focus on the theories of communicative competence and systematically distorted communication, as fundamental issues for a discourse sociolinguistic approach to organizations. Moreover, I will discuss the issue of emancipation through self-reflection, in contrast to Foucault, who argues that changes of discourse always imply changes in power structure, but never destruction of power.

The main aim of communication is to achieve understanding and agreement. If two interactants want to communicate with each other, they have to consider two levels, the level of intersubjectivity, where speaker and hearer talk with each other, and the level of objects, over which they talk. But we can only use sentences as utterances if we know the conditions of possible communication, or in other words, if we have acquired the Universal Pragmatics, a communicative competence, 'to reconstruct the system of rules, once communicative competent speakers form propositions from utterances and reshape them into other utterances'.

Habermas (1971: 114ff) distinguishes between communicative action and discourse. Communicative actions are embedded in a non-verbal context and manifest themselves in normative language-games which are not scrutinized. In discourse, however, we talk about the norms of action themselves, about utterances: 'In discourses we seek to restore, through reasoning, a problematized harmony which has prevailed in communicative action' (Habermas 1971: 115).[15]

How do we distinguish a false consensus from one that is right? Habermas argues that there are no ontological criteria for such a distinction. Thus, we have to be able to find the right consensus ourselves, through the linguistic instruments used in discourse (sic!). Let us try to reconstruct Habermas' argument. A true discourse is measured by whether the discourse contains true statements or facts (as to a case). But when is a statement true? When we can count on the potential agreement of all other speech partners. When is a speech partner competent? When he or she is rational. But when is he or she rational? When he or she has proved by the employment of speech acts that he or she can distinguish between being and appearance and when his or her utterances are truthful. But when are utterances truthful? When the accompanying actions are correct. When are actions correct? When the appropriate rules are being followed, i.e. when the regulatory speech acts are being correctly employed. These rules have intersubjective validity: whether a rule was being followed or not can only be determined by comparison with other utterances (see Habermas 1981, Vol. I: 369ff; Vass 1992: 35ff).

This chain of argument is the basis of the four validity claims of Habermas (Habermas 1970: 372) for an utterance to be free of distortion. At the level of propositional content, a statement makes a logical claim to truth. At the level of illocutionary force, a normative claim is made for rightness, i.e. the establishment of legitimate interpersonal relationships. The third validity claim involves truthfulness in the sense of being sincere about one's utterances. Finally, the fourth validity claim is fulfilled through the comprehensibility of the speakers addressing each other. These four validity claims form Habermas' universal conditions for rationality:

> In this context, truth emerges and is accepted not through a correspondence with an empirical reality, but rather is produced consensually through discursively generated, constraint-free testing of its claims to validity. The product of this 'ideal speech situation' is a rational will that represents common and generalizable, rather than particular, interests. (Mumby 1988: 29)

The ideal speech situation is characterized through the absence of any constraints, so that 'a symmetrical distribution of the opportunities of choosing and practising speech acts exists for all participants' (Habermas 1971: 137). The ideal speech situation thus allows for self-reflection, which we have already identified as a precondition for emancipation. But Habermas argues that we always use the model of the ideal speech situation while communicating, as otherwise communication would be impossible. The ideal speech situation is the 'constitutive condition for possible speech' (Habermas 1971: 141); a comparison of everyday situations with the ideal speech situation where no power relationships exist allows us to detect **distorted communication,** to make transparent the impact of ideology and domination. Undistorted communication thus arises out of the ability of each (communicatively competent) speaker to test rigorously the justifiability of each validity claim put forward by redeeming it discursively (Habermas 1970b: 372). In contrast, systematically distorted communication occurs when the universal, pragmatic norms of the ideal speech situation become subordinated to privileged interests, producing asymmetrical power relationships and resulting in a false consensus about the validity claims made. This is especially true for discourse (in the linguistic sense) in organizations. Normative power exists within an organization when communicative action is distorted through the imposition of interests particular to a certain group:

> A social theory critical of ideology can, therefore, identify the normative power built into the institutional system of a society only if it starts from the model of the suppression of generalizable interests and compares normative structures existing at a given time with the hypothetical state of a system of norms formed, ceteris paribus, discursively. (Habermas 1975: 113)

How then is emancipation possible in organizations? Through the process of self-reflection the emancipatory interest is conceived as the means by which individuals can escape natural constraints in institutional structures. Self-reflection, Habermas claims, can deconstruct the predominance of technical interests, which obscures the self-reflective move in knowledge formation (Habermas 1972: 197ff). Thus, the theory of communicative competence brings the emancipatory interest to fruition: 'It is only in the context of an interest in emancipation that communication can be non-authoritarian and undistorted, producing universally practised dialogue from which our ... idea of true consensus [is] always implicitly derived' (Habermas 1969: 314).

1.5.3 Consequences for discourse sociolinguistics

Discourse sociolinguistics as part of critical discourse analysis pursues the goal of emancipation formulated by Habermas. Through the critique of existing power structures and disorders in discourse in organizations new guidelines for communication are elaborated; news broadcasts become comprehensible, as do new laws (Chapter 4). But, as we shall see when discussing these programmes in detail, the results are of a contradictory nature. For example, more comprehensible news texts are better understood, but only by the group of informants who are well educated and possess experience with textuality and literacy. The other group, less educated people, also understand the texts better, but their gain in understanding is smaller. The gap between the social classes and groups widens, inequality is reinforced. This is certainly not the scenario Habermas had in mind. The same is true in doctor-patient communication. Some patients, those with experience, are able to communicate better; others remain powerless. Moreover, in analysing an attempt to change communication in schools through democratization, my results prove that existing power structures do not change, decisions are still taken by the principals, the upper reaches of the hierarchies. On the other hand, in my study of therapeutic discourse, I show that patients of all social classes do have the possibility of changing their lives, of emancipating themselves, through the self-reflection made possible in this very specific setting.

The above leads us to conclude that Foucault and Habermas are both right or wrong, depending on the perspective; that it depends very much on the specific context in organizations which changes are possible and who has access to and the need to change. As long as structures of organizations do not change, social inequality will not vanish, and changes may actually lead to more subtle patterns of domination, as our example of discourse in schools illustrates. On the other hand, agents are not totally powerless (see Giddens 1988), and some do seize the opportunity to initiate changes in discourse, and thus changes in structures. As discourse socio-linguists, we provide instruments for a less authoritarian discourse. And such instruments may, but do not have to, lead to emancipation. Thus, the results of our studies are important in many ways. First, they make transparent inequality and domination. Secondly, they enable us to propose possibilities of change. And, thirdly, they show the limits of possible emancipation through new patterns of discourse alone.

Notes

1. Habermas follows Alfred Schütz' (1960) conception of 'Lebenswelt' in his methodological considerations.
2. The terms 'institution' and 'organization' are used synonymously because linguistic research talks about institutions, sociological research about organizations (see Mumby 1988, Theis 1994, Giddens 1989, Wodak 1994a, Drew/Heritage 1992).
3. It should be noted here that applied linguistics means something different in Europe than in the USA. Departments of Applied Linguistics, like the one at the University of Vienna, integrate sociolinguistics, psycholinguistics and discourse analysis as well as language teaching. That the European notion is slowly making its way to the USA is visible in the themes discussed at the Association of American Applied Linguistics Conferences over the last years.
4. See Theis 1994, Mumby 1988, Giddens 1989, Drew/Heritage 1992, Boden & Zimmerman 1993, Wodak 1987a, Wodak/Menz/Lalouschek 1989 for recent overviews.
5. Etymologically 'discourse' is derived from the Latin verb *discurrere* ('to run to and from') and/or the substantive variant *discursus* ('divergence', 'melting', 'spreading', with the figurative meaning 'to hold forth about a subject', 'communication about something'). (Vass 1992: 7) The medieval Latin *discursus*, however, apart from 'conversation', 'enthusiastic discussion', also means 'orbit' and '(inter)communication', 'intercourse' (Vogt 1987: 16). Thomas Aquinas (1225/27–1274) is the first to use the term in philosophy. In his work it means something like 'mental deduction'. 'Discursive', that is, by deduction, is contrasted with 'simplici intuitu', that is, by simple

intuition; knowledge through concepts and thinking in concepts is discursive (Eisler 1927: 86). This bipolarity can also be found in Hobbes, Leibniz and Kant, who, after all, is of the opinion that human thought in general is discursive (Kant 1974: 109). Maas (1988) demonstrates that the meaning in everyday language in all western European languages has developed towards 'scholarly deliberation' and beyond that to 'dialogue'.

6. We cannot deal, in this context, with the convergence of developments within text linguistics and discourse analysis. See Vass (1992: 10), Beaugrande/Dressler (1981), Beaugrande (1994).

7. See also Fairclough (1992: 4): 'my attempt at drawing together language analysis and social theory centres upon a combination of this more social-theoretical sense of discourse [in Foucault's sense] with the "text-interaction" sense in linguistically-oriented discourse analysis'. Fairclough continues in defining three dimensions of 'discourse': any discursive event is seen as an instance of discursive and social practice. 'Text' relates to the linguistic analysis, 'discourse' to the interaction, to processes of text production and interpretation. The 'social practice' dimension relates to the institutional context of the discursive event. Any transcript of discourse, according to Fairclough, however, would be labelled 'text'. Fairclough himself is very influenced by Foucault and Pêcheux, but mostly also by Hallidayan linguistics (Fairclough 1992: 55ff).

8. An example of that would be the various guidelines for non-sexist use of language (Wodak *et al.* 1987). By the use of both male and female forms, it is hoped that the consciousness of users will, ultimately, be changed and not only their language use. Making women visible in discourse would, therefore, also result in a different evaluation of women.

9. In this section I have no intention of taking up a position within the immense body of Wittgenstein exegesis, but only of testing the applicability of the central ideas and concepts for a theory of discourse (cf. *inter alia* Monk 1990).

10. The extracts from Wittgenstein are taken from L. Wittgenstein, *Philosophische Untersuchungen/Philosophical Investigations*, trans. by G.E.M. Anscombe, Oxford 1967. For an extensive discussion of CDA see Kress 1993, Fairclough 1992, 1993, van Dijk 1993a, Fairclough/Wodak 1996, Wodak 1994a. Discourse sociolinguistics is viewed as one school in CDA, in which several schools are integrated with very different methodologies and very different theoretical claims. In this section I refer mainly to the theoretical approach in Fairclough/Wodak (1996).

11. Wodak (1994b) explores this development for the domain of doctor–patient communication.

12. Conversation analysis has opted for a research strategy in which only the information that the participants themselves make available is to be evoked by the researcher (Schegloff 1992, Drew/Heritage 1992): 'Invoking social structure or the setting of the talk at the outset can systematically distract from, even blind us to, details of those domains of events in the world' (Schegloff 1992: 127). However, Cicourel (1992: 292) points out some possible limitations of this programme when applied without a critical attitude. The omission of apparent extra-textual information can be problematic to the extent that it obscures information that was at some time relevant to the researcher during the collection and analysis of the material under discussion.

> But if a fuller analysis of participant observation and ethnographic understanding about activities, objects and ideas is desired, and that understanding presupposes prior social experience, and/or technical, scientific, or professional training, then other strategies besides a completely local analysis must be employed. Language and other social practices are interdependent. Knowing something about the ethnographic setting, the perception of and characteristics attributed to others, and broader and local social organizational conditions becomes imperative for an understanding of linguistic and non-linguistic aspects of communicative events. (Cicourel 1992: 294)

13. This is particularly apparent in the studies of doctor–patient interaction and also in the interaction in school committees. In my study of courtroom discourse (Leodolter 1975a, Wodak 1980, 1984, 1985), the negotiation of guilt was focused upon; the guilt stories were constructed in the interaction.

14. All the following quotes by Habermas and Foucault have been translated by John Hampson from the German or French originals, respectively.

15. It is important to keep this distinction in mind. Many researchers quote Habermas or apply his theories wrongly, i.e. they imply that his notion of discourse is the same as in other theories of discourse. But discourse in the Habermasian sense means a very specific kind of communication. The four validity criteria, which I will elaborate later, relate only to discourse, not to communicative action.

2 'What pills are you on now?' Doctors ask, and patients answer

2.1 Introduction

> Patient: Uh, I haven't been here lately because I had to, uh, switch to [Dr] Kaiser for financial reasons and I've been on leave of absence and they can't take me back for a while.
>
> Dr Masters: Uh huh. What pills are you on now?

This relatively harmless-sounding segment of dialogue is a perfect example of one of the primary problems in the interaction between patient and doctor. At first glance, the only problem most people would note in the exchange is a certain insensitivity on the part of the doctor. However, the problem lies deeper than that, and involves basic assumptions about the encounter by each of the participants. This example illustrates a somewhat insidious form of the more general problem of miscommunication between doctors and patients. Miscommunication, disorders in discourse or lack of communication in the medical setting can have grave consequences, from patient dissatisfaction and confusion to non-compliance with medical advice, resulting in some instances, in physical or mental harm to the patient.

Even Foucault (1973) noticed that the change from a more humane to a technological medicine was marked by a change in communicative patterns. Instead of asking 'Why does it hurt, what happened?', doctors concentrate on 'Where does it hurt?' People are thus objectified, not treated as human beings; instead only parts of their body are focused on. (See 1.5.1 above.)

The dehumanization of medicine can be seen *inter alia* in the technical register used in conversation. The medical jargon – as studies have shown (Hein, *et al.* 1985) – is almost never understood by patients even if they supposedly accept the doctor's answers. In interviews with patients after their conversations with doctors, we found that they had not understood the jargon, but had not dared ask the meaning of certain terms. Many patients are afraid to ask questions, fearing that they might get worse treatment 'because the doctors would be angry'. Thus, miscommunication is predictable in such interactions. Why do doctors (or other professionals) use such jargon? There are many reasons: first, medical terms label certain syndromes and symptoms precisely, so that other doctors know what is meant. Secondly, the use of jargon identifies somebody as belonging to an exclusive group, the specific language serving as part of the formation of identity. Thirdly, the jargon demarcates one group from another, it indicates an elite to which you belong only if you have the training and have learnt the language. The medical jargon, therefore, possesses huge symbolic capital, to borrow a term from Bourdieu (1979). Patients who do not understand and do not speak in the same way are discriminated against and excluded, their language is worth far less on the symbolic market (in Bourdieu's sense of the word).

2.2 Doctor–patient communication

Research into doctor–patient communication has generally been based on one of two approaches: the medico-sociological, which focuses on the institution; and the linguistic, which deals with micro-structural aspects of communication. However, the two approaches have rarely been combined in a single study. Aaron Cicourel, one of the founding figures of doctor–patient research, has shown on the basis of selected interviews the advantages of a conversational analysis approach, in contrast to purely quantitative psychological investigations (see Cicourel 1981, 1985). He repeatedly insists that any analysis must take account of the structural framework as well as the different interests of the two main protagonists, doctor and patient.

Contemporary American research is increasingly limited to the analysis of individual types of conversation, for example question–answer sequences and 'accounts'. Since such conversations are studied in isolation from the wider context of the discourse, they can be interpreted only to a certain point (see, e.g., Fisher/Todd 1983, Fisher/Groce 1990, Freeman 1987, Freeman/Heller 1987, Todd 1983, West 1984). However, two findings from recent American work are relevant to the present study and are worth mentioning. Alexandra Todd (1983) describes the clash between the institutional world and the lay world as a 'frame conflict': value systems, the structuring of knowledge, and traditions all diverge and cause misunderstanding and conflict (see above). One common concrete manifestation of this is the fact that doctors typically want to arrive as quickly as possible at a diagnosis, while patients often want to introduce aspects of their biography and also like to know the implications of their symptoms or illness. Elliott Mishler (1984) shows that even research on communication remains in 'the voice of medicine', so that scientific interpretations are made from the point of view of medical knowledge, and signals coming from the patient are ignored. So, he infers, analysis of doctor–patient communication is often biased.

The medico-sociological approach dominated early work in German-speaking countries, and was marred by the absence of the necessary linguistic categories and methodology. At the centre of this research were case histories and conversations during doctors' rounds (see Köhle/Raspe 1982, Strotzka et al. 1984). Current research based on discourse analysis oscillates between two extremes: on the one hand, a mainly application-oriented approach; on the other hand, one concerned with the smallest units of discourse but with no detailed analysis of context (see Ehlich et al. 1989, Spranz-Fogasy 1987). Thomas Bliesener's study of doctor–patient conversations (1982) represents the first serious attempt at defining a particular subsystem of everyday life in hospital, using discourse analysis. The doctors' rounds are broken down into their various components and phases, and individual problems in patients' communication are pinpointed. Here again, however, no genuinely sociolinguistic aspect is introduced: Bliesener does not investigate, for example, whether women and men or old and young patients are treated differently. He does make the important point though that communicative problems will not be solved simply by devoting more time to patients, as the quality of the doctors' approach and of their conversations with patients also need to be improved. In a study on general practitioners, Norbert Hein (1985) shows clearly that there are language barriers between doctors and patients attributable to differences in social class. Patients from a working-class background were treated with condescension. For example, even the proposed treatment for the same symptom (insomnia) was different for working-class and middle-class patients: the former were offered prescriptions for drugs, the latter were referred to psychotherapy. However, in most of these studies, with the exception of Bliesener (1982), the investigated discourse unit was limited to the exploratory interview itself: everyday life at the institution was merely touched upon (for further details, see Cicourel 1981, Freeman/Heller 1987, Mishler 1984, Menz 1991, Fisher/Groce 1990, West 1990, Wodak 1987a).

2.3 Discourse and context: a study of everyday life in an outpatient ward

2.3.1 *Setting and methodology – the context of the institution*

Most of the studies mentioned above were carried out from the 'outsider perspective' – that is, on the basis of preconceived assumptions, specific discourses were extracted from the larger institutional setting and analysed in isolation. The sense of context in relation to the institution and to daily life within it is therefore lost. The validity of interpretations and findings of such studies is limited by the lack of wider contextualization (see 1.4.1 above).

One of the key premises of our study of an outpatient ward at a Viennese hospital was to work from the 'insider perspective': i.e. researchers enter the institution under investigation and spend as much time there as possible to get to know its rules, both manifest and latent. Only after such participatory observation is the systematic fieldwork started, and only then is it possible to decide which methods should be used and how large the sample should be. In short, inside knowledge of the functioning of the institution in question is constitutive for the whole research design (Habermas 1981). In our case, this entailed observing and recording complete morning sessions as a single discourse unit, with discussions with doctors and patients both before and after. On this basis, it was possible to define new, dynamic categories of analysis which can be combined with the traditional categories to help interpret the data (see 1.4.2 above).

To understand the specific context, it is important to realize that the outpatient ward (Outpatients) has low status and prestige relative to the rest of the institution. It is a kind of outpost and among other things serves as a training ground for young doctors, which causes many problems: inexperienced staff often work where experience is arguably most necessary. Hierarchy, knowledge, experience and gender are interlinked in a unique way in the outpatients. Inefficiency, bad organization and bad training are disguised by the propagation of myths, and therefore stereotypes emerge: doctors never have enough time, they are never wrong, and there is simply no better way of doing things.

In this context, 'myth' is to be understood as a second reality, imposed by the dominant groups (Barthes 1974; see also 1.2 above). Events become linked in a quasi-causal way although they are not related to each other. Their connection then seems quite natural, and everybody is supposed to believe in this secondary reality, it is to be taken as given. Every institution is characterized by countless contradictions between manifest and latent functions. For example, university teachers should be as concerned about their students as about their research. In reality, most are under pressure to publish, and often neglect their teaching duties. Myths, then, serve to disguise such contradictions by legitimizing the contradiction and giving it status. For example, the myth says that only scholars who have had much work published make good teachers, and research then becomes a precondition. In 2.6 below we will analyse some of the myths in the outpatient clinic that became explicit in our data.

Seven morning sessions were covered in detail and 83 individual conversations recorded. The age of the patients ranged from 17 to 87 and there were roughly the same number of men and women. Five doctors were observed, three women and two men. The institution itself was cooperative and supportive. However, some problems did arise, especially when doctors were nervous and felt overstretched by the many contradictory demands imposed on them (see Lalouschek *et al.* 1990 for details).

The following questions provided the basic framework for the study:

- Which elements of the context are relevant in the interactive process? Is the setting, for example, more important than the experience and personality of the doctors, or is the influence of each element different? What typical discourse patterns can be identified? Which disorders of discourse become apparent?

- According to Bourdieu (1979: 355ff), the elite possess power and define 'right' (valuable, correct) linguistic behaviour, thus the language of the elite is 'symbolic capital'. How is this capital 'invested', how are differences in knowledge expressed in this specific case? Does a 'frame conflict' in Todd's sense (1983) exist in the outpatient ward? How do doctors exert their power? Which 'power registers' can be identified?
- How are the values and myths of the institution or culture expressed? How are the contradictions between expectation and reality dealt with? Or, to put it more bluntly, how do doctors and nurses cope with their everyday professional life?

2.3.2 Categories for analysis

In dealing with these questions and assumptions, three dynamic categories were found to be of particular importance. First, the emergence of **patient initiatives** (such as asking for information, making complaints or judgements) and the ways in which *doctors deal with them* (for instance by answering, interrupting or ignoring them), bring two conflicting elements simultaneously into play: the doctors' exercise of power and the patients' voices. Secondly, we focused on **doctors' problem-solving procedures**: the specific discursive way in which doctors deal with each problem manifests the intrinsic contradiction between explicit rules, myths and actual events. Also of interest are relationships within the hierarchy: what do doctors know, what do nurses know, how do they relate to one another? Thirdly, the **discursive negotiation and formation of relationships** between doctor and patient were analysed: each time a relationship is established, fundamental features of the management of relationships are applied. For example, if a personal relationship is established, then important rituals of politeness are observed, certain forms of address are used and so on.

2.4 A typical morning session

2.4.1 The institutional context

A male and a female doctor are working together on a particular morning session. Both have just been on night shift and are exhausted. The initial phase is quiet. Then at 11 a.m. there is an announcement over the intercom system to the effect that all cars have to be removed from the hospital car park by 1 p.m. This announcement causes an outbreak of chaos, for it means that the doctors will at some time have to interrupt their work and leave the ward.

2.4.2 Case study 1: the experienced patient

The first patient is 60 years old and has a stomach complaint. He is to be prepared for an operation in the outpatient ward. The problem that the doctor has to solve is one of non-compliance with official procedures: the patient has apparently taken medication on his own initiative. On the basis of Text 1 (see below), it is possible to analyse strategies of problem-solving, as well as the specific power registers used with an 'experienced' patient, i.e. one well used to hospitals and the behaviour of medical professionals. Through an analysis of the macro-strategies, we can identify specific patterns used to cover up a fault in the procedures on the ward which the patient discovers and exploits. At the same time, this discourse is representative of the quiet initial period, when the patients have more space than at the end of the morning session. In order to obtain a deeper understanding of the case, it is important to note that an 'experienced' patient is the subject here.

Text 1[1]

```
11  ⌈ D: as pills from today
    ⌊ P:                  Yes – and yesterday you
12  ⌈ D:                         Well, I hope it works – hmm well
    ⌊ P: didn't give me any at all.
```

* * * * *

```
31    D: well – but that's always – that's only the Lasix 80
32    D: you can get that from us – yes as well
33  ⌈ D: – you know. Or              have you also taken
    ⌊ P:          I haven't taken any – – no
34  ⌈ D: an 80 today as well?
    ⌊ P:          I haven't taken any – till now
35    D: It says here Lasix 80 miligrams – – as a daily
36    D: dose – – on the chart. Lasix 80 – – yes there was
```

37 ⌈ D: a short break. Oh well
   ⌊ P: I didn't get it till – I didn't get it till –
38 ⌈ D: mhm
   ⌊ P: Dr X [doctor's name] was er down here
39 ⌈ D: yes
   ⌊ P: with me you know. Gave me that er – Novarin. Apart from
40 ⌈ D: Yes I see – you didn't
   ⌊ P: that I haven't had any powders – (..........)
41 ⌈ D: get them again till today? – – Yesterday was
   ⌊ P: Got them
42 ⌈ D: very good
   ⌊ P: today and *yesterday* I took one of my own because
43   P: if you remember – I asked you
44 ⌈ D: yes   that's fine – *good*
   ⌊ P: (..........) that I stopped taking those –
45 ⌈ D: fine – you can start taking them again from today –
   ⌊ P: the powders you know.
46   D: because you don't need any more infusions.

The doctor begins with an indirect accusation: he accuses the patient of having taken a Lasix 80 tablet on his own initiative, even though he is prescribed this drug on the ward anyway (lines 31–43). Possibly, the nurses forgot to give the patient the drug, and for this reason he had to fetch it himself. The accusing voice can be detected in the intonation, especially from the emphasis on the words *as well*. In line 33, the patient tries to justify himself, but the doctor does not allow him to take his 'turn'. It is not until line 34 that the doctor actually pauses, enabling the patient to begin his account. In it, the patient reminds the doctor that the doctor had personally instructed him to take his own tablets (lines 42–43). The doctor tries as early as line 42 to interrupt by offering praise and positive comment, but the patient continues. In line 44, the doctor finally manages to interrupt the patient, again with praise, and then terminates the discussion ('fine, *good*'). The doctor's discursive strategy has therefore served two purposes: to cover up the institution's error and to close a potentially embarrassing discussion on an apparently positive note. In the final part of the episode, the doctor redefines reality, prescribes the same medicine again and legitimizes this with new information (lines 45–6). In this way, he resumes his active role in keeping with his position of power.

This episode leads to the doctor being relatively open towards this (experienced) patient. This encourages the patient to take another initiative by asking: 'What's the next step – well, at least here in hospital I mean', to which the doctor replies: 'Well if you if you – can be discharged – as far as the ulcer's concerned – from the surgery wing, which will clearly be soon' The doctor responds in more detail to questions concerning the patient's stay in hospital, a strategy that serves to block further non-medical questions. So openness and personal relationships are possible, but only up to a certain point: that is, as long as they remain within the frame determined by the doctor.

However, when the patient takes a third initiative and complains again about the ward: 'I was prescribed the Malox – but I never got any. And that's only one example (..........) first of all that.... But now – now I know if you don't ask', he is praised ('That's right') but then the doctor abruptly changes the topic and asks: 'So when did you have breathing problems – would you tell me about it?'

Text 1 (cont'd)

111 ⌈ D: – yes
    ⌊ P: What's the next step – well –
112 ⌈ D: Well if you
    ⌊ P: at least here in hospital I mean
113   D: if you – can be discharged – as far as the ulcer's
114   D: concerned – from the surgery wing, which will clearly
115 ⌈ D: be soon   That we could perhaps add
    ⌊ P: Yes That's what I meant
116   D: on – a short stay *here* – until
117 ⌈ D: the pulse rate's settled down again a bit.
    ⌊ P: Is it possible for me –
118 ⌈ D: In the surgery wing?
    ⌊ P: to stay there?   Yes – is that OK?
119 ⌈ D: Well, I mean theoretically that's OK – but but
    ⌊ P: that's OK
120 ⌈ D: whether Dr X [doctor's name] will allow it, you know –
    ⌊ P: whether he'll allow it
121   D: if you're not a surgical case any longer. –
122   D: We'll have a word about it – yes. At any rate
123   D: there's no question of you being discharged yet. – But
124   D: the liver results have gotten better – and the
125   D: pulse has gone down a bit – yeah?

* * * * *

```
141   P: It's like this – well – what's it called Mulox or something
142 ⎡ D: Malox yes
      ⎣ P:    I was prescribed the Malox – but I never got
143   P: any. And that's only one example (..........) first of all
144 ⎡ D:              mhm
      ⎣ P: that. (..........) But now – now I know
145 ⎡ D:                                        That's right
      ⎣ P: if you don't ask (..........)
146   D: So when did you have breathing problems – would you
147   D: tell me about it?
```

* * * * *

```
183 ⎡ D:                     Yes – it'll be sent up.
      ⎣ P: Will it be sent up?
184 ⎡ D:       Yes?              X [surname]
      ⎣ P: Doctor – may I ask your name
185 ⎡ D:       Not at all.          Goodbye.
      ⎣ P: Thank you          Goodbye.
```

The same pattern as in Text 1 (above) is repeated, but here it is much stronger as the experience of the patient becomes a little too threatening. However, the doctor maintains his formal manner and takes his leave politely. A relatively close relationship has been established, there has been no clash between different 'worlds of knowledge', yet the doctor has had to work hard to maintain his authority, using several strategies (interruption, rationalization and change of topic). One particularly subtle aspect was the discursive strategy of combining praise and mitigation and/or a change of topic, a clever 'packaging' of power.

2.4.3 Case study 2: the inexperienced patient

The second patient enters the ward at 9.45 a.m. She is considered a difficult patient because of her age (87). She is not prepared to take off her hospital gown as there are men present. Here there is a real clash between values and generations coupled with a total lack of 'experience' on the part of the patient. Through a micro-analysis of this case study, it is possible to make explicit the systematic interaction of different aspects of discourse (speech acts, particles, forms of address, socio-phonological realizations) in the process of the adaptation of the patient to the institution.

Text 2 contains extracts from the beginning, middle and end of the examination.

Text 2

1   D2: Right we'll have to take off the gown too
      P: (..........) don't

2   D2: Why not? – We *are* in the hospital you know. Right –
           now then

3   D2: let's sit down here shall we?
      P: /quietly/   (..........)

4   D2: *Right* take off the gown please.
      P: Gown – but I've

5   D2:   take it off please – the gown. We've
      P: got nothing under the gown.

6   D2: got to do an ECG. Right   No one's
      P: (..........) Gown

7   D2: looking – – well – it's only the doctor

8   D2: – isn't it.   He's allowed
      P: The doctor can look – but

9   D2: to look isn't he – right let's sit down here

10   D2: shall we.   exactly
      P: Sometimes he even has to look (..........)

11   D2: Right – tell me, which was the broken arm?

* * * * *

64   D2: She keeps wobbling around – – *now just lie still*

65   D2: *Don't keep wobbling around – or the ECG won't work*

66   D2: *quite still – just relax*, OK   Good – – right
      P: All right – yes.

67   D2: that's fi:ne.

* * * * *

221   D2: But she's sore *everywhere* – – she's sore

222   D2: everywhere.   *Does it hurt there too?*
       P: Ah: yes /sighs/   (..........)

223   D2: Ah, not there – only the back and there it does hurt,
           doesn't it
      P: it's OK

224   D2:   Yes – and there?
      P: It hurts there.   Well – I can feel it –
         but

225   D2:   not too bad.
      P: it's bearable.

The doctor makes four attempts to get the patient to take off her gown. The first is in the form of an indirect speech act using a childlike form of address ('we'll have to ... [muß ma]'), which I refer to as *pluralis hospitalis*. Then the doctor tries to persuade the patient to comply with her wishes by rationalizing the situation ('we *are* in the hospital ... [wir san ja im Spital]'), but again without success. After a structuring signal ('Right'), the doctor makes a fresh attempt, this time in the form of a polite but firm request ('take off the gown please [so tun Sie das bitte ausziehen]'), using a more direct but still distant or polite form of address and a socio-phonological switch into standard Austrian German articulation.[2] Finally, when the patient still refuses to oblige, the doctor repeats her request ('take it off please – the gown [Ziehen's das aus bitte – das Hemd]'), the imperative form indicating the more peremptory nature of this attempt. She reinforces this with a technical explanation, which the patient does not understand. As the patient still fails to remove her gown, the doctor tries to reassure her that no one else is looking other than her (male) colleague (lines 6–7); the particle 'Right' is intended as both concluding signal and reassurance. The patient begins to give in, although she still does not seem to be totally convinced (line 8). The doctor picks up this more positive sign, echoing the patient's remark that 'The doctor can look' and switching to the same dialect as the patient, which helps to bring the two closer together. She follows this up with a further request, softened by the reassuring particle ('OK [gell]'). The patient again repeats 'Sometimes he even has to look', as if to convince herself, referring to the male doctor, and the doctor confirms this before changing the topic with the structuring signal 'Right [So]'. Then the actual examination begins.

Later in the examination, the doctor is unable to control her irritation with the patient and begins to shout at her (lines 64–6). A direct request occurs, which is realized in standard German. Three more demands follow before she resumes a calmer, reassuring tone (line 67). The final section of the discourse (from line 221) is polite and gentle, and the patient is more subdued. The patient is the subject of the discourse but is referred to in the third person (line 221): this is a common pattern, but it causes considerable uncertainty among patients as it is not clear who is under discussion. Only the use of a direct question (line 222) makes it clear that at that point it is the patient herself who is being referred to and that a response is required. Finally, the patient concedes that 'it's bearable': a sign that she has, at last, adapted to the institutional frame.

The doctor's manner with the patient ranges from a gentle approach through stiff formality and impatience to harsh authority. These changes are indicated by the character of the various requests (direct and indirect), the different forms of address, and the switches in socio-phonological style. The patient is given little in the way of discursive orientation other than the particles 'OK', 'right' and so on, which are used to express reassurance and as structuring signals (beginning or concluding topics). There appears to be a clear correlation between these indicators, and certain patterns emerge: for example, indirectness of request is associated with *pluralis hospitalis*, the use of dialect and certain particles.

The doctor's behaviour is a form of exercising power, but it also reflects a conflict that is caused by a number of factors. It is the first time for her that a professional conversation with a patient is being recorded. The patient is considered 'difficult', as her 'uncooperative' behaviour slows the examination down, and the doctor has difficulty in analysing her fears. The case is therefore seen as a disruption of the normal routine, it conflicts with institutional expectations. As a result, no close personal relationship is established between doctor and patient. Helpful explanations and information are not forthcoming precisely when they are most needed, and even when the doctor does attempt a more personal approach, it is characterized by 'motherese' (see Wodak/Schulz 1986) and *pluralis hospitalis*. This only serves to reinforce the difference in power and the patient's assumed mental inferiority. The frame conflict and the language barriers (the differing use of standard Austrian German and Viennese dialect) separating the two participants render cooperative face-to-face communication virtually impossible, the disorders in discourse are dominant, and in the end the patient falls silent.

2.4.4 Case study 3: the disruptive case history

The following patient was being treated for the first time by the hospital, i.e. she was not sent from an inpatient ward, but went direct to the hospital and was sent to the outpatient ward by the duty doctor. The patient is 30 years old, female, Yugoslavian, speaks good German, and has experience of hospitals, from her colostomy operation. The reason for her hospital visit is a feverish infection which has persisted for some time and bronchitis. In the course of the examination, several disruptions occur which turn the quiet morning into chaos and render the two doctors in the outpatient ward helpless.

1st disruption

The senior doctor enters Outpatients. The male doctor D has been waiting for him to discuss the many 'interesting cases'. The senior doctor SD, however, is 'taken over' (lines 12, 13) immediately by the outpatient nurse S1, who needs him for the ergonometry test, which is actually the responsibility of a senior doctor. S1 wants him first to complete the examination which has just begun (11). D is clearly disappointed at this turn of events ('Alright then' (14)). (D2 is the female doctor.)

```
10    D:  /phones/ senior doctor – – you
      S1: right – I need    /SD enters/
11    D:       We've got a few discussions
      S1: the senior doctor.
12    D:
      D2: OK let's talk about it – let's talk about it
13    S1: Let's do the ergonometry test first of all.
      D:  Do the ergonometry test then
14    D:  Alright then (..........)
15    S1: We've still got four ergonometry tests to do.
```

2nd disruption

First-aid cases are treated every other day. This 'duty day' is subject to many potential disruptions, from emergency cases to unforeseen duties, and the number of patients cannot be calculated in advance. The female doctor D2, who had not been expecting a duty day, turns to the nurse S3 who has more knowledge and experience, and has to alter her expectations of a peaceful morning session.

```
30    D2: I always thought we had duty day every other day
31    D2:       No – doesn't matter.
      S3: No – – –
```

3rd disruption

The senior doctor comes in again and takes away the good blood pressure gauge without the male doctor D, who is doing the examination, noticing. He thereby disrupts the course of the examination and underlines at the same time his position of power.

4th disruption

Following the 3rd disruption there is a difficult conversation between the two doctors on duty, D and D2: since the beginning of the examination, D has been on the phone to a senior doctor of another ward about the diabetes check-up of the previous patient, and has noted down the results and therapeutic instructions without informing D2. He has taken over the medically relevant, and therefore interesting, tasks – i.e. he notes the results and has detailed discussions on the phone with the senior doctor – without including the female doctor D2 in his actions. She gets angry and feels excluded.

130	D:	X [name of senior doctor] has just taken it
	D2:	Where is it (blood pressure gauge)?
131	D:	/takes away the results/ – – aha
	D2:	May I have a look
132	D:	I've got
	D2:	at that as well – before you take it away
133	D:	everything – I tell you everything – there's so much lying around here
	D2:	because I wanted
134	D:	– – what I wrote?
	D2:	to know about it as well
135	D:	noted it down after checking with the senior doctor
136	D:	X [name] – ah diabetes – what then?
	D2:	No, not what you've written (..........)
137	D:	yeah, that's what was said – leave it – it's
138	D:	set well enough. Leave it and only – once a week
139	D:	three times daily the blood sugars. [have to be tested]

The other doctor D2 reacts against being treated in this way ('May I have a look at that as well' [131, 132]), emphasizes her equally strong medical interest ('because I wanted to know about it as well' [133,134]) and becomes indignant when the doctor begins to read the results to her word for word ('after checking with the senior doctor X' [135]), i.e. refuses to hold a professional conversation.

5th disruption

For the first time the male doctor D comes in on the examination which is being done by D2, the other doctor on duty. A misunderstanding occurs between D and the patient: the patient is there as a result of her lung condition and not, as the doctor assumes, because of an intestinal complaint.

190 ⌈ D: Yeah, but why is she coming to us – now
     ⌊ D2:   Yes, for an

191 ⌈ D2: assessment
     ⌊ P: because I've still got a temperature – and

192 ⌈ D: Yes, but, I mean, you know – you were –
     ⌊ P: I can't

193   D: you're sure, aren't you – in which department

194 ⌈ D: were you?
     ⌊ P: What's that got to do with the colostomy bag?

195   D: No no – that's what I'm saying – look, that's – that's

196   D: difficult of course. Ah – diarrhoea – antibiotics of

197 ⌈ D: course – it all plays a role somewhere
     ⌊ P: I'm not here because of

198 ⌈ D: Yes, because of your temperature
     ⌊ P: diarrhoea – I've had diarrhoea since yesterday

199 ⌈ D2:   temperature and your
     ⌊ P: but my temperature – temperature I've had anyway

200 ⌈ D2: lung condition
     ⌊ P: That's got nothing to do with (..........)

The doctor D is impatient and wants to terminate this examination which, in his opinion, does not belong in Outpatients and is holding up his work, i.e. is causing an additional disruption (190, 193, 194). He signals distance by not talking with the patient, but instead talking about her ('Yeah, but why is she coming to us – now' [190]) and standing next to her without properly acknowledging her, i.e. by greeting her. Instead he starts talking to her without any introductory remarks (192). In case study 2 (see 2.4.3 above), we have already encountered the most distant style of communicating with patients, namely talking about them in their presence. In such situations, the patient is objectified and excluded from any symmetrical relationship.

6th disruption

There then follows a sequence of accusations based on the previous misunderstanding (D having taken the symptom of diarrhoea for granted although it had not been mentioned, either by the patient, or by D2):

206   D: Mainly because of the lung condition at first
207 ⎡ D: I thought – the diarrhoea is not
    ⎣ D2: so acute – that's what you told me. Drug resistant
208   D2: yeah, well – probably both
209 ⎡ D: diarrhoea
    ⎣ D2: No, I didn't actually say that – you
210   D2: read it. So far I haven't said anything to you about
211 ⎡ D: well? – I heard it – as I was on the
    ⎣ D2: diarrhoea
212 ⎡ D: telephone – it was about diarrhoea
    ⎣ D2: I didn't ask her then at all

7th disruption

The intercom announcement already mentioned (see 2.4.1) interrupts the emotionally loaded situation. Reaction to this disruption, which affects the whole of Outpatients, is increasingly dramatic. First, the intercom message is ridiculed and incorporated into the medical discourse:

271 ⎡ D2: Oh God, that just can't be true
    ⎣ D: (..........)
272 ⎡ D2: At 1:00 p.m. today   /laughs/   yeah
    ⎣ D: Not that – but at 1:00 p.m. (..........)
273   D2: but we (..........) but we won't get out of here – we didn't
274 ⎡ D2: get in   what a joke
    ⎣ D: I'm going outside
275   D2: – right – yeah lung – basic displacement
276   D2: the left one looks to me to be higher than the
277   D2: right one. Can't displace it as well

While the doctor removes blood from the patient, he has time to consider the consequences of the intercom request:

309	D:	/to P/ can you move your watch away a bit? - - Oh no
310	D:	and I've got my course at one o'clock – I don't
311	D:	think I've been to the course for three weeks
312	D: D2:	And now the car again – where Hey perhaps we could go there earlier
313	D: D2:	should I put it Okay, we'll just leave it there
314	D:	mmh – there's one. – – Is there a thinner one [needle] than
315	D:	the black one – is the green or the yellow one thinner?

The hectic character of the situation transfers to the waiting patients and to the whole of outpatients:

350	D: D2:	good And they've all still got to be looked at yet – or what?
351	D: D2:	Why did you have to come now yeah (..........) how many
352	D: D2:	yeah – enough more for God's sake

This sequence is typical of behaviour under stress and duress. An event which had been quite normal is now seen only in the light of its potential to further burden or disrupt. The situation becomes emotional. The medical reports of the patients still waiting to be examined, which have remained untouched irrespective of the order in which they were submitted, suddenly become 'still got to be looked at'. The number of patients, which had not been important to the doctors before, now – in the light of the length of the previous examinations – becomes a threat: thus D2 asks, 'How many more for God's sake?' The daily routine of Outpatients, i.e. that a large number of patients have to be seen within a particular period of time, is suddenly seen as a complete surprise by the doctors, and as a considerable challenge to their authority, too. This leads to the whole situation becoming uncontrollable and unpredictable, with the doctors not knowing how to cope with these 'new' events. The burden becomes heavier still, thus militating against any action that might bring about a solution to the situation.

2.4.5 The final stage

Not surprisingly the final stage of the morning session becomes hectic and full of tension, the examinations are significantly shorter and follow-up discussions abandoned altogether. Approaches from patients are ignored and a general sense of distance between patients and staff prevails. In the penultimate examination an ECG is refused, even though the patient should have had one, as the machine does not work straight away. In the end, the doctor appears to be concerned only with his hunger. He says: 'I'm going to die if I don't get something to eat soon'.

2.5 Summary

The texts with their descriptions and analyses show clearly how the external situation influences the (verbal) behaviour of the doctors vis-à-vis their patients as well as each other. It also shows how interruptions, disruptions and burdens are directly imported into the conversation and then simply left there, unprocessed and unresolved, since the disharmony, – the so-called 'routine chaos' – is not accepted emotionally or cognitively. The doctors seem only to react, to be passive; internal and external factors alone seem to define the conversation, and they feel like victims of the circumstances. A more meaningful approach to the disruption, such as perceiving it as routine and part of everyday life, would not only help dispel the 'myth of harmony', but also reduce internal pressure on the personnel and facilitate a more flexible approach to the whole situation.

During quiet, relaxed periods such as the start of the morning session, the doctors too are relaxed and friendly with the patients: conversations last on average 16 minutes, as do the post-examination discussions and those among the doctors themselves. The doctors respond to questions and requests for an explanation from the patients – even if the answers are not always 'patient-oriented' – and sometimes the doctor goes beyond simply answering the questions. Purely medical explanations and humorous observations do not accompany only positive assessments. The unburdened external situation is transferred directly to interaction with the patients and a predominantly relaxed, friendly atmosphere is created except in case study 2.

As soon as an element of disruption occurs, which in this particular morning session happens to be during a somewhat complicated examination, there is a sudden change in the verbal behaviour of the doctors: the patient discussions become shorter (on average 9 minutes). There are no further detailed explanations of the results, nor any post-examination discussions. Patient initiatives are not encouraged and are interrupted. It is noticeable that the number of patient initiatives is minimal. The tense situation is clearly felt and has a direct effect on the verbal behaviour of the patient, just as the relaxed atmosphere of the early morning session virtually prompted patients' initiatives. Uncooperative and problematic patients are treated differently by the doctors, and are implicitly accused of causing additional disruption and burden in the outpatient ward.

The results of the morning session, taken as an example, are typical and can be applied generally to events in Outpatients. Many of the burdening factors, such as the unpredictability of events or parallels between the examination and training situation (doctors are experts and pupils in a training situation at the same time), can be easily recognized through their disfunctionality and corrected by implementing suitable organizational methods. However, there is no hint of change; indeed, the institutional insiders often themselves contribute to an increase in the already heavy burden. It would therefore be appropriate to ask which behavioural strategies, expectations and patterns of interpretation of the institutional members contribute to the contradictions which become apparent in this situation and institution (see below).

2.6 The myths of the outpatient ward

2.6.1 *The functionalizing of contradictions*

The analysis above has shown that conversations and interactions in Outpatients are highly complex processes: i.e. examination, treatment, advice, teaching, learning, organization, reorganization and telephone calls occur simultaneously. Shift doctors, senior doctors, professors, head doctors, senior nurses, outpatient nurses, ward nurses, trainee nurses, orderlies, porters, ambulance personnel, service personnel and, finally, patients come and go. Treatments and examinations take place one after the other, almost without a break.

These overlapping processes lead inevitably to contradictions, and accumulation of roles, and to role conflicts between those involved. The creation of myths is one strategy to cover up such contradictions. These myths serve to give the contradictions a function which stabilizes the system and maintains the formal institution of Outpatients (see 1.2). In addition, they enable the members of the institution to give meaning to contradictory role expectations and conflicts, and thereby apparently overcome them. The following passages illustrate some of the strategies and behavioural patterns of the institutional insiders, which support these myths.

2.6.2 The myth of the undisturbed, predictable process

A session in Outpatients is a highly contingent event. The course of the mornings is unpredictable due to the many disturbances, such as acute emergencies, priority patients, the squeezing-in of patients, and the occurrence of single, unexpected events (intercom announcements, the absence of personnel, machines breaking down). There is a high degree of uncertainty.

One strategy for coming to terms with the instability of the system is expecting the processes to be predictable and uniform, e.g. hospital personnel share a myth of the ideal examination event. Those involved in the examination perceive the ideal, normal process of being cleared for an operation, say, as the following:

- The patient is called in (by a doctor or a nurse).
- The patient undresses and lies down on the bed.
- One of the two doctors present does the examination.
- The patient puts his or her clothes back on and returns to the waiting area.
- The examining doctor dictates the results to the other doctor, then discusses them with him or her; or the examining doctor writes the results himself or herself.
- The next patient is called in.

This kind of examination process is however a rare exception. The real examination process as it happens daily is quite different, as our case study 3 (the disrupted examination) illustrates:

- The nurse calls in patient P1.
- P1 removes his clothes and lies down on the bed.
- Doctor enters and discusses the results of a previous patient P2 with second doctor.

- Doctor calls for the medical history of P1.
- P1 is greeted.
- Second doctor begins the examination.
- There are no notes on P1 to be found.
- Doctor looks for nose drops.
- A doctor enters and asks the second doctor about another patient (P3), D2 answers and continues with the examination.
- The nurse brings an X-ray of an earlier patient P4 to be checked over.
- The ECG has to be repeated since it was not correctly in position.
- The results are not in order.
- The telephone rings, the nurse answers the call.
- The orderly enters to take P1 for his operation.
- Doctor leaves to fetch the senior doctor SD.
- Second doctor, P1 and the orderly wait.
- Doctor returns, the senior doctor is busy.
- The nurse calls doctor to the telephone: another patient, P5, should be slipped in.
- Second doctor listens to P1's chest with the stethoscope.
- A taxi driver knocks on the door and looks for a patient, P6.
- Two porters announce patient P5, who was booked in by telephone.
- Doctor dictates the results to D2.
- Doctor again leaves to fetch the senior doctor.
- Second doctor tells P1 about the waiting time.
- The nurse is on the telephone.
- Doctor and the senior doctor enter.
- Technical discussion between D, D2 and SD.
- The telephone rings, the nurse answers the call.
- A patient, P7, enters and looks for registration.
- The professor enters, talks with SD and takes patient P5 with him.
- Second doctor and doctor finish writing their results on P1.

As we have seen, the normal process is not quiet, uniform or undisturbed, but is characterized by disruption and uncertainty and is in a constant state of flux. Everyday life in Outpatients is a continuous juxtaposition and confusion of different actions and discussions. *The disrupted process could trenchantly be described as the normal process (there is order in the disorder).* As long as doctors and nurses in Outpatients do not accept that disruption and interruption are part of the normal routine and that an undisturbed, quiet examination is an exception to the rule, then they will continue to interpret each disruption as an affront and feel overburdened. Due to their idealized expectations, they are completely at the mercy of the situation, which they cope with only through dismissive comments and grumbling.

44   D: OK – they're making me rush around like crazy

* * * * *

65 ⎡ D: oh: well: I thought it was
   ⎣ D2:   yeah, yeah – you have to
66 ⎡ D: yeah, yeah, everything – you
   ⎣ D2: get it all wrong, don't you
67 ⎡ D: have to do everything all at the same time
   ⎣ D2:   three things
68 ⎡ D: that's the great thing with us
   ⎣ D2: all at the same time

In moments of stress, everyone grumbling together – about the situation, the wards or people in higher positions – seems to have the function of relief and solidarity.

2.6.3 The myth of efficiency

As we have seen, the interruption, i.e. the disruption of the examination taking place, is an overriding characteristic of all examinations. These interruptions are caused on the one hand by outside events such as telephone calls, intercom announcements or through people entering (doctors, nurses, orderlies, patients, etc.) and, on the other hand, by the doctors themselves: during the examination of one patient the results of previous patients are discussed and telephone calls made, people leave the room, and nurses and doctors gossip with the senior doctor who has entered. Many of the interruptions are necessary and form part of the routine of Outpatients (outside telephone calls, giving priority to emergency cases, waiting for the senior doctor regarding difficult decisions); other interruptions could be avoided. One thing is clear: efficient work is impossible under such conditions; anger, disappointment and dissatisfaction are automatic reactions. One of the ways in which doctors themselves contribute to the lack of effectiveness is by discussing the results of previous patients, in the presence of the patient under examination. This so-called time-saving concurrent event regularly causes further disruption, mis-understanding and disorders of discourse. This again gives rise to confused conversations and misinterpretation for those patients present since they normally do not know about this habit, nor do they have technical medical knowledge, which might help them understand that part of conversation which really concerns them.

35	D2:	Good morning. What's her name? /to P/
	P:	X. [patient's name]
36	D2:	/looks at the results folder of P, in which D is writing /
37	D2:	/to D/ you know, she's quite anaemic – the patient 27,9 and has
38	D2:	got quite a high blood count
	D:	Ahha Hmmm
39	D2:	mean potassium – he's prescribed her Kalioral
40	D2:	but I really do think that a blood bottle should be
41	D2:	written down – 'cause that's certain – I don't
42	D2:	know about a larger operation – hmmm? – –
	D:	hmmm – we'll call
43	D2:	/murmurs/ (..........)
	D:	X [senior doctor's name]
44	D2:	/to P/ So – you come from here – from which ward?
45	P:	births

* * * * *

120	D2:	No, I think that was
	P:	was that anaemia thing about me?
121	D2:	about the previous patient – disturbed you a bit – no no:
	P:	hmmm
122	D2:	we haven't actually seen anything of you at all

2.6.4 The myth of time

The disruptions, interruptions and unpredictable events add to the pressure on the medical staff and their sense of being overburdened, which already exists in their relationship with the doctors through the latters' implicitly contradictory double role of examiner (i.e. expert) and pupil (trainee). At the same time this overburden and the constant pressure of time for staff in Outpatients have the

function of legitimizing the meaning, importance and necessity of
their work and actions. After all, there exists the role stereotype of
the doctor constantly on call and thus permanently under pressure
of time.

One paradox of the tense, stressful situation in Outpatients is
waiting for the senior doctor: if, during the examination, the results
point to clearance for an operation or discharge being questioned,
then the senior doctor must be called upon to make a decision; and
this means – as in the following case – that everyone must wait for
the senior doctor.

```
110     D2: /to D/  Mhmm – so if you think that there's only
111  ⎡  D2: One result here – – then you're wrong
     ⎣  D:  yes well – – well please
112  ⎡  D2:        yes right –
     ⎣  D:  send him to X [senior doctor's name]
```

Doctors and nurses, in accordance with the myths of time, efficiency, and predictability of the process, begin to bridge the waiting
time with various tasks (sorting card indexes, heading results
sheets), or they start looking for the senior doctor. Only the patient,
who was not informed, is unclear about why he must continue to lie
there half-naked and why, all of a sudden, the focus of general
interest has turned away from him. After a few minutes waiting he
begins to question the situation:

```
337  ⎡  P:  Can I put my clothes on again?
     ⎣  D2: No, you've still got to wait
338     D2: a little for the senior doctor – you know – because we
            said
339     D2: your ECG was negative – – and you're anaemic
340     D2: OK
```

Despite being late, the long-awaited explanation (from the doctor)
finally arrives. This leads us to the question of how patient and
doctor differently experience the situation and to what extent
institutional insiders consider it necessary to inform institutional
outsiders about processes and events. Sometimes, they do not seem
to care about, or at least understand, the worries of the patient.

2.6.5 *The myth of collective knowledge – the reality of insiders and outsiders*

The complex process of the outpatient ward should be daily routine for the insiders of the institution, i.e. the doctors and medical staff. They know the procedures and their way around the complicated network of tasks, people and hierarchies, and the areas of responsibility of the institution.

Those who are least familiar with the procedures are the patients, for whom the outpatient ward exists. It is normally impossible for patients to penetrate these complex processes, find their place within them or interpret them correctly, or really understand their meaning and purpose. Previous studies of doctor–patient communication show clearly that a lack of information for the patient is a central part of this type of communication: lack of information about current procedures and future action, about the illness, technical expressions, results or therapy. The lack of information for patients is often so extreme that they are not aware of why they are in Outpatients at all, what will happen to them or when, or what operation they may face.

1 P: This is an examination, isn't it?
   D: An examination, yes:
2 P: for an operation – yes
   D: well, well not quite – here it says
3 P: yes –
   D: that you've already *had* an operation another
4 P: I don't know
   D: operation   you see – I don't know
5 D: either – nothing here about it.

In addition to a lack of technical medical knowledge, the patients, if they do not have much experience of hospitals, i.e. some 'insider-knowledge', do not have the complex knowledge of the doctors and nurses about the routine procedures of examination, nor do they know that interruptions and overlapping activities and discussions are part of the normal process or that, in most cases, only part of the actual interaction in the room where they are present refers to them.

It is noticeable in the discussions that we have examined that the doctors never explicitly tell the patients when the focus of the conversation is changing, i.e. when the examination is interrupted. This frequently leads to misunderstandings and disorders: patients react to statements not directed at them, and associate the results of previous patients with themselves, which makes them worried, even afraid; they attach the wrong importance to a question which, because of interruptions and the apparent confusion of events, is inadvertently asked more than once, and they end up feeling insecure.

The verbal routines of the doctors and nurses, with whose help the patients *could* come to terms with the interruptions and changes, are so minimal – if they occur at all – that they scarcely offer them help in coming to terms with the situation.

The inability of institutional insiders to see trouble spots ('organizational blindness') in their own organization often reaches the extent that they forget that, for many patients entering a room, it is probably a completely new situation, or at least one which they do not often encounter and where they have no routines to help them adjust to or find their way in the organization (e.g. case study 2, the old woman who did not know that she had to take off her gown).

The provision of essential information during the examination would help the patients become more cooperative and understand the examination. This would not require more time as other time, currently wasted on miscommunication and misunderstanding, would be saved. Also, doctors do not have to discuss other patients during the examination of one patient; they could find time between patients to catch up. If the senior doctor has to be fetched, this again could be explained to the patient, he or she could be asked to wait outside, and another patient could be seen in the meantime. When the senior doctor arrives, all unresolved problems could then be discussed at once. The prevention of unnecessary misunderstandings and disruptions would be a first step towards really effective interaction and easing the pressure of time.

An analysis of the whole morning (in contrast to taking small sequences of conversation out of context) allowed us to diagnose typical inefficient behaviour patterns which could be changed relatively easily, even inside the existing structures of medical institutions. Discourse analysis, therefore, provides an important means for medical practice to make changes in behavioral patterns which, though relatively small in themselves, have considerable impact on the quality of professional work and on the well-being of patients. In this case, changes would probably lead to a better treatment of the patients, not only a more subtle domination (see 1.5.1 above).

Notes

1. **Transcription symbols** (after HIAT [Halbinterpretative Arbeitstranskription] see Ehlich/Switalla 1976):

[	line brackets to show that people are speaking at the same time
D	male doctor
D2	female doctor
P	patient
(..........)	inaudible passage
–	break in intonation
– –	short pause
/sighs/	non-verbal feature (example)
a:	long vowel (example)
you	word spoken with emphasis (example)
.	falling intonation
?	question intonation
* * * * *	lines omitted

2. The phonological situation in Vienna is actually diglossic: standard Austrian German is spoken by the upper classes, Viennese dialect by the lower classes. Also, we find gender-specific variations. In between these two extremes, a whole range of variants exist. Austrian German has significant differences from High German, represented in *Duden* as the prescriptive norm. (See Leodolter 1975a, Moosmüller 1989, Dressler/Wodak 1981, Wodak-Leodolter/Dressler 1978, etc. for details on linguistic variation in Vienna.)

3 Hierarchy or democracy? Power and discourse in school committee meetings

3.1 Introduction: 'school partnership'

In this chapter I shall examine the relationship between power and interaction in schools, in the light of results obtained in a recent study of three Viennese schools. The study registered, described and interpreted the presence and frequency of specific discursive mechanisms in the interaction between participants in committees established by law as part of the Austrian 'school partnership'. At the same time, selected qualitative analyses of discourse data will serve to illustrate in detail how certain power relationships function (for details of the whole study see Wodak/Andraschko 1994). Another interesting aspect which I will not elaborate here (see Wodak 1994c) are the leadership styles enacted by the three female principals of the schools. In contrast to some recent studies (Helgesen 1990), I am not able to find a more cooperative and less hierarchical style when analysing discourses of these three women. I would like to suggest that in this case institutional culture, myths and routines predominate, the hierarchy in Austrian schools is so rigid that flexibility and other modes of leadership are not possible. Thus, again, context-oriented research proves that also gender-specific behaviour patterns are subject to certain settings and dependent on other variables.

'School partnership' is a concept contained in a 1985 Austrian law concerning the participation of teachers, parents and pupils in school affairs. The law also contains provision for School Welfare Committees (SWC), Parents' Associations (PA), and school and class forums (SF and CF respectively) to embody this partnership.[1]

There is, however, a basic tension between what the law is seeking to achieve and the context (institutions) in which the means are expected to operate. For how can a 'school partnership', which prescribes equal opportunity, participation and democracy for its deliberative bodies, be reconciled with the rigidly hierarchical Austrian school system? In my view, it cannot, and to demonstrate this theoretically as well as empirically I would like to consider briefly the notion of power and examine how power may be exerted, expressed, described, concealed or legitimized by the social and communicative interaction in institutions such as schools – in short, how power 'works' and how power structures frustrate possibilities of democratic participation.

3.2 Power, control and institutions (schools)

3.2.1 *Power and hierarchy*

Van Dijk (1989: 19ff) summarizes the interaction between those with and those without power as follows: the person exerting power (A) is in control of the cognitive conditions such as wishes, plans, etc. of the other person (B); at the same time, this control is also accepted by B. Social power is thus largely indirect and occurs through mental processes, for example, evaluating the information necessary to plan and execute (communicative) actions. The cognitive process itself, of course, also provides the means of coming to terms with and resisting this power. In other words, exerting power is not simply a form of action, but a form of social interaction which has to be more or less negotiated each time. In our study of power relations within schools (Wodak *et al.* 1992), we attempt to take account of this complexity by using detailed discourse analysis to uncover the dialectics of power and helplessness, of controlling and being controlled, of activity and passivity in institutions (see Habermas 1981). Those factors typical of an institution – rules and regulations, assigned roles and a rigid internal organization such as the hierarchy of positions and the ritualization of procedures (see 1.2 above) – collide ineluctably with structures designed to promote democratic control.

The bottom line here is the legitimacy of power. The free and secret election of persons to committees is the principal means for acquiring this legitimacy. In institutions with democratic procedures, legitimacy is usually determined on the basis of the majority of voters. But this is possible only if the ballot is really secret, and the political climate promotes reliable information about the electoral candidates. Moreover, it is essential that oppositional views and candidates exist. These conditions, however, are frequently absent in Austrian schools. As Schneider (1977) points out, in addition to being based on reward, force or attraction, power can also be based on the knowledge of facts, i.e. power based on information and power based on the selection of information; on legitimation through a position in the hierarchy of an institution; or on the control of a given situation, e.g. presidency in a legal sense. Persons in higher hierarchical positions in an institution or school, e.g. headteachers, automatically have direct access to relevant information and are therefore in a position of control based on the selection of information (see below Text 2); similarly, they have a legal presidential function in committees such as the SWC or SF and therefore have control of those interactive situations as well.

Even when the available means of participation, criticism and debate in school committees are really used as intended, their efficacy is by no means assured. Beyond this difficulty, however, is the far less tractable problem of the authenticity of the consensus itself, for the shared perception of which structures ought to exist and how and why they ought to work is also analysable in terms of power relations. Methodologically, our investigation was required continually to relate several sets of questions to various levels of discourse, in an effort to examine the efficacy of the procedures, i.e. the correspondence (or lack of correspondence) between the stated objectives of the law and mechanisms to institutionalize supervisory control; the way in which a consensus about and within given procedures was obtained; and whether the outcome of the procedures validated or undermined (in the opinions of the participants) either the controlling structures themselves or the democratic premises underlying them.

3.2.2 *Power and interaction*

What then is the relationship between discourse and social power? How do discourse and power relationships interact, and how is power exerted in terms of language? Foucault (1977), Bourdieu (1987) and van Dijk (1989) all interpret social power as discursive control: who has access to the various types of discourse, who can and cannot talk to whom, in which situations, and about what. The more powerful the people, the larger their verbal possibilities in discourse become. This is particularly apparent in institutional discourse. In such situations, persons entering the institution from outside, for example patients, clients or parents, do not act on their own initiative, but react by answering questions, listening and providing the information sought. In the institution, persons who determine the interaction occupy an institutional role (doctor, teacher or headteacher, etc.) and their language behaviour is consequently supported or legitimized by the existing institutional power. These factors beget and stabilize frame conflicts and miscommunication in institutions (see Chapter 1).

Persons with power determine the course of the interaction, the issues discussed, the choice of words, and can determine verbal discourse by allowing, continuing or interrupting individual contributions. Such persons also determine the beginning and end of the interaction. In addition, the interaction can be manipulated by passing on information selectively, or, in other words, withholding information that could undermine those in power. This issue is a central theme in our illustrative qualitative analysis of interaction sequences (see 3.5.3 below).

Power structures in schools can thus be illustrated by looking at the gap between the minimum information that parents require in order to make a reasonable judgement on the issues under discussion, and the information actually provided by the school authorities. In the examples I have chosen – those involving electoral procedures – it is obvious that most parents were insufficiently informed not only about the agenda of the ongoing subcommittee but also about the candidates and the voting procedure. The democratic procedures laid down were thus in themselves inadequate, and the chairpersons and headteachers successfully managed to promote their preferred candidates and own agendas.

Text 1: Grammar School Parents' Association

The PA was run according to its constitution, i.e. reports by the committee, the accountant, approval by the committee, elections as well as a decision on the membership fee. Each voting and electoral procedure requires information about the activity and financial situation of the PA, and also about the organization of the association, its active representatives and the relationship between PA and school committees such as the SWC. In other words, one of the main functions of the PA is to provide parents of children attending the school with information about the school and its activities.

The chairwoman and treasurer delivered their detailed reports on activities and projects such as refurbishing the school building, school events, the purchase of teaching materials, as well as those prospective undertakings to be financed by membership fees and donations. This information was presented clearly and comprehensively, and complied fully with legal requirements. Indeed, provision was even made for 'new parents' sitting in the hall, i.e. parents of first-year pupils,

> Ch = chairwoman
> Tr = treasurer

1	Tr: about the membership fee –
	Ch: yes! OK.
2	Tr: I want to mention – for the new people. I would like to
3	but I think there were a couple of new parents here who
4	probably don't know yet. Er – for example it remains at
5	160 schillings and say you've got children at other
6	schools and one here – then of course you only pay half
7	and if you've got several children at this school (..........)

The situation was different, however, regarding information about organizational issues of the association. Precise information about who would stand for election in the first place, how the list of electoral candidates would be put forward, how a person could put him- or herself up for election, was not forthcoming. Only the names and functions were read out:

> L = Mr L. from the election committee

1	L: Madam counsellor – members of the parents'
2	association and er parents. It is my task again to put
3	forward one of our election proposals to this hall and
4	then I shall ask you to make your choice as appropriate
5	– er – I shall perhaps first of all read out the names –

This led to the following situation: the election of the committee takes place after the chairwoman (Ms K.) has delivered a detailed report on projects that have taken place or are planned by the Parents' Association:

L   = Mr L. from the election committee
H   = headmistress
X   = female member of the audience

1	L:	I would like to request the hall, well, I shall read out the
2		name of the the chairperson alone, then I shall ask for a
3		vote to be taken, as I said, er Ms – K. has been put
4		forward as she has put in more and more hard work for
5		many years now. That she should
6	L:	continue to do this work. Those in favour please hm
	H:	There! That's her
7	L:	raise your hand /pause/ Well – that's
	X:	Who's that? Ms K.? I don't know her
8	L:	the lady who gave a report – yes. Crosscheck.

Owing to a basic lack of information, the person who had been talking for the past 30 minutes had not been clearly identified as the chairwoman of the PA. Thus, it is hardly surprising that procedures concerning the election of a new committee were all passed without any opposing votes, because the candidates were not even known to everybody.

3.3 The data of the study

3.3.1 *The origins of the study and the collection of data*

One aim of our study was to measure the actual workings of the statutory committees in the various types of school against the explicit intentions of the school partnership law which established them. It was necessary to collect comprehensive data in order to be able to describe the setting and meaning of the committees in the individual schools and to illustrate issues of more general interest. Thus, the data covered not only committees such as the SWC (School Welfare Committee), the SF (school forum) and CF (class forum) but also meetings of the PA (Parents' Association). In addition, we decided to include situations from the everyday life of the school (such as classroom interactions, teachers' meetings and parents' evenings) in order to understand the structures of the institution as a whole. Data were collected at three different types of school – a grammar school (GS), a secondary modern school (SMS), and a junior school (JS) (a primary school for children from six to ten) – to enable us to compare how school committees dealt with problems particular to their type of school. Finally, in our study, we employed methods of participant observation, tape recordings and written reports as well as in-depth interviews (in the concluding phase of the project) with selected people involved. This took considerable time and was very labour-intensive. The frequent presence over a long period of time of those collecting the data in the schools meant that the subjects of the study became used to their observers. It was therefore possible to observe undistorted communication since it is more difficult to control one's own behaviour over longer periods of time (cf. Wodak 1986a).

The transcription of the cassette recordings was carried out concurrently with the collection of further data in several phases. This approach proved to be particularly reliable when dealing with interactions involving more than two people (cf. Lalouschek/Menz/ Wodak 1990). Initially, a rough transcription of all the communicative situations, or of selected passages, was made; the observers then edited the transcriptions. The intermediary transcripts were suitable for rough analyses of the discursive data. A further, more refined transcription was necessary for micro-analysis.

3.3.2 *Data overview*

3.3.2.1 *School statistics*

The following statistics obtained from the headteachers give a sense of each school's demographic profile:

Junior School (JS)
  1 headmistress
  1 psychologist
 14 core teaching staff (13 female, 1 male)
 13 additional teaching staff (religion, foreign languages, etc.)
 14 classes with a total of 179 girls and 171 boys (total 350), incl. 72 foreign pupils (20.6%)

Secondary Modern School (SMS)
1 headmistress
1 psychologist
28 core teaching staff (22 female, 6 male)
1 accompanying teacher
10 classes with a total of 137 boys, 90 girls (total 227), incl. 153 foreign pupils (67.4%)

Grammar School (GS)
1 headmistress
56 core teaching staff (45 female, 11 male)
40 additional teaching staff (all on fixed contracts)
23 classes with a total of 226 boys, 279 girls (total 505, no foreign pupils)

3.3.2.2 *The data*

Committees
GS School Welfare Committee (SWC)
SMS school forum (SF)
JS school forum (SF)
JS class forum in 2nd form (CF)
JS class forum in 3rd form (CF)

Parents' Associations
GS Parents' Association (GS PA)
SMS Parents' Association Committee 1 (SMS PAC 1)
Parents' Association Committee 2 (SMS PAC 2)
JS Parents' Association (JS PA)

Daily School Life Situations
GS: classroom teaching
teachers' meeting
parents' open day
school meeting
SMS: classroom teaching
parents' evening for 2nd form
parents' open day

3.3.3 *The complexity of the data and consequences for the analysis*

In contrast to many previous studies on institutional communication (e.g. Lalouschek et al. 1990), these data consist of interactive events that differ from one another in many respects but are related on a number of different levels. On the one hand, the school partnership committees we recorded owe their existence to, and observe the guidelines elaborated in, the school legislation; on the other hand, communicative situations such as teachers' meetings, open days for parents, and classroom teaching derive their forms and procedures from the institutional framework of the school.

The collection of data took place in three different types of school, and so there were influences specific to the type of school and to the individual school itself. Examples include different leadership styles among the headmistresses (Wodak/Andraschko 1994) and the various possibilities of involving parents and pupils in classroom and school activities. One problem was the high proportion of children or parents in the SMS with no or little knowledge of German. Two final factors of some significance were the proportion of girls to boys and the subjects taught.

The sections that follow contain an overview of the individual meetings, the issues discussed, the length of the dialogues and contributions, and those features influenced by the type and geographical location of the school. The subsequent qualitative text analyses illustrate how important events in the meetings (i.e. voting behaviour and approval of the agenda, which we used as an indicator of 'democratic attitudes') were 'managed' in verbal terms. On the basis of qualitative text analyses it is possible to estimate the extent to which these patterns were dependent on the type of school, the meeting, or the people present, and to indicate the consequences of the different strategies employed in the course of the meetings, i.e. which aspects of participation and partnership were realized, which thwarted.

3.4 A quantitative overview

The first overview of the data is a rough quantitative description of the length of contribution of each individual, the issues and motions raised by them and the participation of the forum present. This representation is summarized in the Tables 3.1, 3.2 and 3.3, which were drawn up according to the type of school (JS, SMS, GS) and are divided into committees, Parents' Association meetings and other settings.

3.4.1 Observations on the individual categories

3.4.1.1 Length of contribution

In every setting and in each type of school, the main time contribution was usually claimed by the president, for example the headmistresses or the chairwoman of the Parents' Association,

Table 3.1: Junior school

		SF	PA	CF (2)
Number of those present	total	48	48	22
	male	8	8	6
	female	40	40	16
Length of meeting (mins.)		8	21	88
Contribution (%)	president	19	67	8
	officers	81	19	12
	forum	–	14	80
Issues (according to agenda)	total	2	8	3
	organizational	1	7	1
	educational	1	1	2
Issues (additional)	total	–	–	3
	organizational	–	–	2
	educational	–	–	1
Motions	total	3	4	1
	passed	3	4	1
	rejected	–	–	–
	deferred	–	–	–
	passed unanimously	3	4	–
	not passed unanimously	–	–	1
Initiatives from forum	total	–	5	59
	relevant to issue	–	5	56
	independent of issue	–	–	3
Discussion		–	–	+

SF – school forum; PA – Parents' Association committee; CF – class forum

Table 3.2:   Secondary modern school

		SF	PA1	PA2
Number of those present	total	30	25	19
	male	4	3	4
	female	26	22	15
Length of meeting (mins.)		33	41	58
Contribution (%)	president	70	20	11
	officers	15	37	47
	forum	15	43	42
Issues (according to agenda)	total	6	9	6
	organizational	3	9	3
	educational	3	–	3
Issues (additional)	total	–	3	–
	organizational	–	3	–
	educational	–	–	–
Motions	total	1	9	2
	passed	1	9	2
	rejected	–	–	–
	deferred	–	–	–
	passed unanimously	1	9	2
	not passed unanimously	–	–	–
Initiatives from forum	total	8	23	31
	relevant to issue	8	21	31
	independent of issue	–	2	–
Discussion		–	+	+

SF – school forum; PA1–PA2 – Parents' Association committees

followed by the co-chairperson. In committees where the head-mistresses were not also presidents, they tended to occupy the floor more than the presidents. The time available for contribution by other officers or others present was minimal in comparison. As the following description of issues discussed shows, participation by the non-officials present, when it did occur, was mostly around an issue of general interest. Yet large segments of many meetings take place with no verbal participation by the non-officials in attendance.

Table 3.3:   Grammar school

		SWC	PA	TM	SM
	total	10	87	49	38
Number of those present	male	4	25	10	7
	female	6	52	39	29
Length of meeting (mins.)		58	117	60	28
	president	43	23	55	54
Contribution (%)	officers	40	50	–	–
	forum	–	26	45	46
	total	4	8	6	1
Issues (according to agenda)	organizational	3	7	4	1
	educational	1	1	2	–
	total	1	–	1	–
Issues (additional)	organizational	1	–	–	–
	educational	–	–	1	–
	total	4	7		
	passed	4	6		
Motions	rejected	–	–		
	deferred	–	1		
	passed unanimously	3	5		
	not passed unanimously	1	1		
Initiatives from forum	total	42	21	24	44
	relevant to issue	39	20	21	43
	independent of issue	3	1	3	1
Discussion		+	+	+	+

SWC – School welfare committee; PA – Parents Association Committee; TM – Teacher Meeting; SM – School Meeting

3.4.1.2 *The individual types of school*

Secondary Modern School (SMS)

The headmistress claimed for herself a large proportion of the time used (e.g. 47% head vs. 11% chairperson), not only in the SF where she was president but also in the PA committee meetings to which she was invited. This is in part to do with the fact that the chairwoman's role is mainly a structural one – she reads out, for example, the motions and 'administers' the vote. The contributions of the headmistress, on the contrary, contain considerable background information about motions regarding financial support of various activities and projects, everyday life in the school, general statements about difficulties facing the school, the problem of the high proportion of foreign pupils and so on. The headmistress was frequently invited to speak by the chairwoman.

Junior School (JS)

The opposite was true of the JS. Here, the chairwoman claimed for herself most of the time used for discussion in both the JS PA and the SF; she took over the structuring of the meetings and offered additional information, ranging from uses to which PA membership fees might be put, to a description of a planned project in a class.

Grammar School (GS)

The GS offered a more complex picture. In a setting in which the president was responsible to the headmistress, the headmistress claimed for herself a large amount of the time used for dialogue, underlining her hierarchical status. In the GS PA, the chairwoman took over the procedural and substantive parts of the agenda. The long monologue of the headmistress in this setting resulted from a report she gave on the issue of sixth-form reform which was a separate part of the meeting. The functions of headmistress and chairwoman were therefore divided according to the meetings and were more clearly separate than in the other schools.

3.4.1.3 *The issues*

In general, it can be said that purely organizational issues predominated in all settings in all schools. Even educational issues, such as films for Third World Day or the school library, were seen from a purely organizational aspect, i.e. that of financial support.

Educational issues were dealt with primarily in more 'open' settings, e.g. in the CF of the JS, which dealt exclusively with a project on 'oral reports'. One exception was the SF of the SMS (a more restrictive situation). There, issues such as school field trips, theatre productions and stopping the school project 'heterogeneous German' were examined on their educational merits. Even this positive aspect is qualified by the fact that the headmistress and one female teacher simply reported on the issues, and there was no discussion involving the rest of the meeting. Eighty-five per cent of the time used for discussion was taken up by the headmistress and this one teacher; the remaining time was spent on a total of eight requests for additional information from participants in the meeting.

Those few issues addressed in the committees and in the PA meetings that were not on the written agenda were purely organizational, dealing with school holidays and additional financial support for events or the school library. Issues where decisions were necessary became the subject of motions.

3.4.1.4 The motions

The motions were a fundamental and therefore particularly important area of participation. Active participation is normally characterized by a discussion of the motions on the agenda and by a voting behaviour where votes against or deferring an action, or outright rejection are as legitimate a form of behaviour as unanimous acceptance. In our study, however, the picture was completely different: in the settings that we examined, not one of the 31 motions was rejected and only one motion, at the GS PA, was deferred.

Votes against the motion were cast on only three occasions. The issues concerned the smokers' room (in the SWC), an increase in the PA membership fee (in the GS), and the extension of a school project on 'oral reports' (at the parents' evening in the JS). The other motions (27 in all) were carried unanimously.

3.4.1.5 Initiatives from the forum

The forum comprises those in attendance who, unlike the president, do not have the right to speak first. The category verbal initiatives includes such activities as asking questions, making comments, providing descriptions, etc. These develop the issue under discussion or introduce new topics. At first glance, there seem to have been a considerable number of participant initiatives in both the GS and SMS, suggesting the active participation of those present. On closer examination, however, these initiatives turn out to be connected predominantly to one issue only, while the questions and interjections dealt simply with the agenda. If one were to examine the connection between the individual issues and the initiatives, the picture would be as follows.

Five issues were discussed in the SWC of the GS. Seventy-five per cent of the initiatives from the forum referred to the smokers' room. In the GS PA, eight different issues were discussed and seven motions put forward. Initiatives by members of the forum referred almost exclusively to the issue of refurbishing the classrooms. In the PA 1 of the SMS, 12 issues were discussed and nine motions put forward. The initiatives were concerned essentially with a buffet and the Christmas bazaar.

In some of the settings, the forum gave hardly any verbal response: in the SF of the SMS, seven different issues were discussed in 33 minutes. In total, only eight initiatives were put forward by the 28 participants (not counting the chairpersons). The situation in the JS was even more extreme: the SF, in which two issues were mentioned and three motions put forward, was conducted with no verbal participation by the 46 people in the forum (not counting the chairpersons). In the PA GM, eight issues were discussed and four motions put forward. Only five initiatives came from the 46 participants.

Thus, if there had been no issue of general interest on the agenda, such as the organization of the buffet or the classrooms, the forum would hardly have participated at all. Most discussion time was limited to a few of those present, often either the president or someone occupying a high position in the hierarchy; the various issues were dealt with predominantly from an organizational point of view; there were practically no debates with an educational content; and the voting behaviour was stereotypical and passive.

3.5 The qualitative analysis: selective information as a means of power

3.5.1 Objectives of the analysis

The linguistic analysis of different situations in which the legal potential of partnership at school is put into practice, is concerned with what really happens in concrete everyday situations. We shall first present the possibilities laid down by the law, and then examine which opportunities are utilized by individual participants in a given situation, and which not.

The first stage of the analysis is to describe the manifest linguistic processes visible on the surface. Each step in the organization and structuralization of meetings, such as greeting, introducing the subjects, presenting the agenda or putting forward a motion, requires that the appropriate verbal behaviour be realized. This realization is contingent on the person, function and role of the speaker, on the situation and its function, and on the composition of the others present, and exerts a varying influence on the direct course of interaction, hence also on the verbal behaviour of the other participants.

This leads to the second stage of the analysis, recording the processes on the **microlevel**, i.e. the latent, implicit levels of meaning and relationships (see Chapter 5). Each form of verbal behaviour contains encouraging, restrictive or preventive elements vis-à-vis other participants in the interaction, and is thus also an expression of dealing with relationships and power. So the micro-analysis of verbal strategies is intended to show what influence different forms of linguistic realization have on the relationships between the interactors, whether they reproduce, consolidate or possibly even artificially re-create existing power structures; whether they are apt to enable equality of action and conduct above and beyond the existing hierarchical barriers; or, finally, whether the possibilities of co-determination provided by the law are utilized at all.

In another stage of this study it will be necessary to investigate the interactive handling of discrepancies wherever *contradictions* appear between formal or legal provisions and real behaviour, or between equal rights and institutional hierarchy. As I have demonstrated elsewhere in examinations of linguistic behaviour in institutions, the specific and repeated emphasis of harmony (a myth) ('We are all in the same boat'), for instance, also serves to disguise existing conflicts or real power structures, and prevent discussion (cf. also Lalouschek *et al.* 1990).

An important scientific prerequisite for this kind of micro-analysis is a precise and careful transcription of the tape-recorded material using an elaborate transliteration system (HIAT after Ehlich/Switalla 1976). The transcription, above all of interactive situations involving more than two speakers, e.g. interaction in the classroom, interaction in committees or meetings, is arduous and time-consuming as all the strands of conversation, which often run parallel, have to be kept apart.

3.5.2 *The structure of meetings and categories of analysis*

Every meeting can be divided up into the following model, with clearly identifiable stages (macro-strategies):

Step 1: Salutation
Step 2: Introducing/reading the agenda
Step 3: Presentation of general information
Step 4: Putting forward a motion
      4.1 Presentation of the motion
      4.2 Discussion of the motion
      4.3 Vote on the motion
      4.4 Discussion of the vote
      4.5 Acceptance, rejection, deferral of the motion
      (4.1–4.5 may be repeated any number of times)
Step 5: Miscellaneous items and discussion
Step 6: Concluding remarks. Thanks

This structure suggests the following categories of verbal realization, which form the basis for analysis of the entire textual material:

Macro-strategy	*Linguistic realization*
Salutation, introductory remarks	
Reading of the agenda	all the information
	part of the information
	no information
The motion	
• Presentation	subjects
	explanation to create solidarity
• Discussion	initiates discussion
	prevents discussion
• Move to vote	neutral
	open
	persuasive, suggestive
• Behaviour when voting	silence
	hand signals
	verbal
• Discussion, votes against	assertion

	justification
	relativization
	rejection

General discussion

Presentation by the chair	open, encouraging
	closed, preventive
Treatment of the call for	acceptance
discussion	non-acceptance (explicit/in
	silence)
	demand

Let us look at some examples for the macro-strategies: Once the subjects have been presented, the chairperson usually calls on the other participants to ask their questions. The call can be worded in such a way that it can encourage, hinder, or prevent questions. Text 2 is an example of an encouraging formulation:

Text 2: SMS school forum

```
        H  = headmistress
400     H: Have I forgotten anything? – Help me. –
           Have I forgotten anything? I don't know.
           Do you have any – questions – for me or to put to
           the class teachers. – Could we close the
           door. – Do you have any questions. (...........)
           Is there anything you want to know?
```

The headmistress expresses her call for questions in a neutral way 'Do you have any questions for me', but also in a particularly open form 'Is there anything you want to know?' This form of linguistic realization indicates to the participants that there is enough time for questions and that questions are also encouraged.

Text 3, is an example of a preventive formulation.

Text 3: SMS Parents' Association committee

```
        Ch  = chairwoman
        H   = headmistress
482  [  Ch: OK. I think that was it, wasn't it? No more
        H:     Yes.
483     Ch: Comments or suggestions.
```

The chairwoman ends the meeting with the words 'OK. I think that was it' (line 482). Then with the negatively worded statement 'No more comments or suggestions' (lines 482–3), she indicates that she does not expect any more. This linguistic realization of the call to ask questions makes it difficult to ask them, or even prevents them altogether.

3.5.2.1 Salutation

In text 4, as in most cases the greeting went hand in hand with introducing the researchers present and asking the forum's permission for them to use the tape recorder. Recording started with step 2, introducing and reading the agenda.

3.5.2.2 Introducing/reading the agenda

Introducing the agenda is the duty of the chair and serves to inform everyone about the procedure and content of the meeting. For some meetings the agenda was made known beforehand, whether by means of a notice at the Grammar School textbook conference, which takes place once a year, in the fall, to decide which textbooks should be used during the school year, or leaflets distributed to the students for the Grammar School Parents' Association general meeting. Such a procedure gives participants more time to prepare.

According to our data, an explicit and detailed announcement of the agenda is not typical of committee meetings. The introduction also includes a description of the first item on the agenda.

Text 4: JS school forum

```
        Ch  = chairwoman
        T   = teacher
065   Ch: Yes. Eh ... next. I would like to ask the headmistress
066       because this evening is also. Eh ... the school forum.
067       That you take the chair. And now we must ask
068       whether you agree with the nominations for teacher and
069       parent representatives for each class
070  [  Ch: For the school forum committee.
     [  T: /(..........)/
```

The JS class forum on the subject of 'verbal assessment' is opened by the form mistress as shown in Text 5.

Text 5: JS class forum

```
        Tf  = female teacher
035     Tf: I would like to begin this evening by (..........)
036         Three weeks ago I did an assessment with the children –
037         each child assessed him or herself (..........)
```

This step of announcing the agenda and getting it approved constitutes, even if it is neglected, part of the knowledge of the insiders in the institution. This can be seen in Text 6.

Text 6: GS teachers' meeting

```
        H  = headmistress
010     H: Always a problem. OK I have finished with my
011        administrative duties and according to the agenda
012        would now request Prof. X [doctor's name] I haven't
013        asked if you agree with it – but nobody noticed – to say
014        something about EDP in the middle school.
```

The fact that a step was not taken is immediately blamed on the teachers at the meeting because they failed to insist on a vote on the agenda. This raises the fundamental issue of the distribution of power at meetings, an issue that will recur throughout this chapter. To what extent and by what acts do participants in the meeting contribute towards the chairperson's ability to structure the course of the meeting according to his or her own desires? In this case we have a waiver of the right to be informed about the agenda and to vote on it (power needs impotence; cf. Strotzka 1985, Wodak 1989).

Without a rundown of the agenda, additional subjects can be introduced, only at the end of the meeting – if at all. Furthermore, there is no possibility of including these items at the outset so that they also receive due consideration. Hence, the treatment of such subjects is dependent on the forcefulness of the participants and the attention they are given by the chair. Not making the agenda explicit is also a form of giving selective information. The less information the participants have at their disposal, the slimmer their chances of playing an active role and initiating a critical discussion. If there is no agenda, the course of the meeting is determined interactively, as shown in Texts 7 and 8.

Text 7: SMS school forum

```
         H  = Headmistress
         Tf = female teacher
  056 [  H:  And 4B will join in – I mean
       [  Tf7: (..........)
  057    H:  The skiing course – so they would prefer to go skiing.
  058        What have we/to TF4/dealt with? – By way of positive
  059        things?
```

Text 8: School Welfare Committee

```
  550     H:  I might write that into the minutes as well – I think
  551 [   H:  that's about it or is there anything else? Please
       [   Tf3:                      Oh yes, Oh yes, there's the (..........)
```

Here a teacher asks for financial support for a film show on the subject of the 'Third World'.

```
  633 [   H:  We'll put up a struggle. Are there any more problems
       [   Tf1:                                       Yes, one
  634     Tf1:     Yes, mhm (..........) simply a point of information
```

In the discussion that follows this teacher presents in great detail the problems caused by changes in the arrangements for looking after the children in the afternoon and the resultant financial burden on their parents.

Such sequences convey, at first glance, the impression of lively, open and 'unbureaucratic' meetings. With questions such as 'What have we dealt with?' or 'Are there any more problems?' the chairpersons indicate their willingness to include the forum's suggestions, queries and problems in the meeting. In this context it is striking that in the case of the school forum meeting the lengthier subjects are broached only when the headmistress raises them and are not actively introduced by the teachers, even though the items have been specially prepared for the meeting.

Not explicitly including these subjects as items on the agenda has the disadvantage of having meetings of unforeseeable length and content. They cannot focus their attention on the agenda and many items run the risk of being deferred for lack of time or being inadequately handled because other participants do not have enough information. The chairperson is in the position to determine whether certain subjects are discussed only briefly or not at all. Another disadvantage is that it depends on calls from the chair whether such subjects are addressed at all, or whether participants can assert themselves in the interaction in such a way that their questions or concerns become discussed by the meeting, even if not introduced by the chair.

Only once in our data is the agenda presented in full detail and a vote taken on it – in the PA general meeting at the Grammar School. A few days earlier, the agenda had been given to the students to pass on to their parents.

Text 9: Parents' Association general meeting

	Ch	= chair
001	Ch:	Once – Perhaps I may read the items for those who
002		recently (..........) eh (..........) have only glanced at it or
003		didn't get an agenda. Or where there was a
004		communication breakdown. First, eh, welcome,
005		approval of the agenda, appointment of an electoral
006		committee. Chairperson's report – Treasurer's report –
007		Auditor's report and acceptance of accounts; election of
008		a Chairperson; election of parent representatives for the
009		school community – committee decision on membership
010		fee for the school year 1989/90 then we have planned a
011		break with – a small buffet prepared by the 6th form –
012		donations are towards the trip after exams are over.
013		Then Ms X [name of head] has declared herself willing
014		to talk about the new curricula for the junior and senior
015		schools and the organizational – eh – organization,
016		reforms of the senior school and to explain the current
017		problems caused by the restructuring and finally we
018		have planned a discussion on miscellaneous items. Ah
019		do you agree with this agenda? – Ah, are there any votes
020		against? (..........) Then we approve it. (..........) Then I'll
021		come straight to the next item, the appointment of the
022		electoral (..........)

When we compare this presentation of the agenda with the list of topics dealt with at the meeting, it is striking above all that the legal requirements and the planned talk by the headmistress are named as items, but that the domain of motions and votes, the domain in which parents can participate actively, is not mentioned with regard to voting on the agenda. The very subjects 'skiing, flea market' and 'repair fund for the classrooms' meet with general interest at the forum, and find expression in many suggestions on the part of the forum at this point in the meeting.

So the presentation of the agenda is detailed, but lacks substance at critical points. In principle, such a constellation could allow considerable scope for those parts of the meeting to take a concrete course and the active participation of those present.

The announcement 'and finally we have planned a discussion on miscellaneous items' (lines 017–018) indicates to the participants that, at this stage in the proceedings, discussion is desired. However, being presented as a separate item on the agenda for the end of the meeting, it is unclear whether discussions may or should take place during the meeting too. Moreover, in view of the planned length and variety of content it is doubtful whether a specific subject and issue-related discussion could come about in this form.

3.5.2.3 *Move to vote*

More or less deliberate influencing of the outcome of the vote is also connected with the linguistic realization of the call to vote. Let us look at some textual examples.

The most neutral wording, one which allows, so to speak, both 'yes' and 'no' as answers, is a split question such as 'Who is in favour? Who against?'

Text 10: SMS Parents' Association committee

```
        Ch  = chair
        Sm  = secretary (male)
        Tr  = treasurer (male)

      ⎡ Ch: A motion, please, for the picture frames?
 404  ⎢ Sm:                        Picture frames, OK.
      ⎣ Trm:                       Vote.
```

405 ⎡ Sm: Vote. Who is in favour, who is against?
    ⎣ Trm: Ms M. will do it.

Most moves to vote are formulations such as 'Do you agree?' Such
a question is not really neutral as it expresses on expectation of
agreement and so exerts pressure for an affirmative answer.

Text 11: GS Parents' Association general meeting

018   Ch: Planned miscellaneous items. – Eh, do you agree with
019   this agenda? – Ah, are there any votes against? (..........)
020   then we approve it – then I'll come straight

Text 12: school forum

        Ch = chairwoman
        P   = parent
065   Ch: Yes. So. Eh (..........) next. I would like to ask the
066   headmistress because this evening is also. Eh the school
067   forum. to take the chair, please. And now we must all
068   ask if you agree with the teachers and parent class
069   representatives who have been
070 ⎡ Ch: nominated for the school forum committee.
    ⎣ P: /(..........)/

Leading questions such as 'You'll approve that again?' or 'Anyone
against it?', as in the following extracts, show an even greater bias:

Text 13: SMS Parents' Association committee

        Ch = chairwoman
        P   = parent
        Pm = male parent
019   Ch: The . . . the next thing is the down payment for the
020   headmistress 800 shillings a year – You'll approve that
021   again?

    ⎡ Ch:Yes. Anyone against it? The down payment is
022 ⎢ P: Yes, certainly.
    ⎣ Pm3:   We need a motion

Text 14: SMS Parents' Association committee

> H = headmistress
> Pf = female parent
> Ch = chairwoman
> Pm = male parent

046	H:	Wait, we need a few more and I would strongly request
047		you to support the motion. I really need it. – Yes
048	H:	Then you can do it straight away. That, of course
	Pf:	fine! /hahaha/
049	Ch:	Nobody's asked – there are
	H:	Nobody's against it; I think. Ha?
050	Ch:	10 pieces? at 80 shillings. Is anyone against it?
	H:	10 pieces
	Pm3:	10
051	Ch:	OK. Super.

The influence of the headmistress on the acceptance of the motion, 'I would strongly request you to support the motion' (046–047) is quite explicit, and her verbal behaviour in the School Welfare Committee meeting is especially revealing. In this body she holds the chair, but no right to vote. Nevertheless, or perhaps for this very reason, she gives her personal opinion before every vote, regardless of the subject.

Text 15: GS School Welfare Committee

> H = headmistress
> Tf = female teacher

551	H:	Is that all or is there anything else? Please.
	Tf3:	Oh yes, Oh yes. There's something. There's
552a	H:	Yes
	Tf3:	To mark Third World Day on 1 December
552b	H:	Yes
	Tf3:	Colleague P. would like to show a film and also do a
553	H:	the Third World Day is the first December
	Tf3:	Fund drive and eh asks the SWC for financial
554		support
555	Tf3:	totalling 1000 shillings (..........)
556	H:	Personally I've no objection – That's your affair.

$$557 \left[\begin{array}{ll} \text{H:} & \text{We have the budget for school events – so} \\ \text{Tf:} & \text{Yes Yes Yes Yes} \end{array} \right.$$

$$558 \left[\begin{array}{ll} \text{H:} & \text{OK. It's approved} \\ \text{Tr:} & \text{Yes} \\ \text{Tf3:} & \text{Then I have a second point} \end{array} \right.$$

Before a vote is taken on the motion about financial support, the headmistress intervenes with the statement 'personally I've no objection' (555). She then appears to relativize her position with the following remark 'That's your affair' (556). Of course, her direct influencing of the other participants' opinions still holds.

She acts in a similiar way when a vote is taken on the main subject of the School Welfare Committee meeting, a smokers' room:

Text 16: School Welfare Committee

364	H:	The question is can we now take a vote that we leave it
365		as it is – so that we don't end up sitting here forever
366		talking about an issue we have discussed so often
367		anyway. I have no vote. So I ask who is for the motion
368		that in this building the room under my office and the
369		separate part of the courtyard over there are open to
370		smokers in the breaks at 9 10 11 and 12. I ask for 1 2 3
371		4 5. – 1 2 3 4. So 5 to 4 – it's carried.

The headmistress calls for a vote. With her subsequent negative evaluation of the previous discussion of this subject 'sitting here for ever' (365) and 'discussed so often anyway' (366), she makes clear what she considers an acceptable outcome. In this case, too, she relativizes her own 'vote' explicitly with the remark 'I have no vote' (366). Such a prophylactic expression of opinion is a form of control that has become routine and can be observed in conferences and other meetings, irrespective of their precise setting.

3.5.3 *Who possesses information?*

As studies on communication in institutions, above all in hospitals, have shown, information issues are an important indicator of power structures, since the privileged possession of information bestows power on the possessor. When information is withheld, institutional outsiders can easily be excluded from communication and therefore from participation in an event. PAs are seen as an essential link between the institution of the school and the 'outside world' of the parents. For this reason it seemed advisable to use the PAs to examine areas in which, and issues about which, schools informed parents, where they did not inform parents, and how requests for additional information were handled (see Text 1 above).

A similar situation to the one discussed in Text 1 occurred during the voting on who should represent the PA on the SWC: despite the question at the beginning of the meeting about the abbreviation SWC, it was not appreciated by those present that vital information was missing. Although mention was made of the importance of this decision prior to the vote, those present were offered no basic information about the SWC, a body whose decisions could significantly influence internal school events:

Text 17: GS SWC

<pre>
         Ch = chairwoman
         H   = headmistress
         U   = Mrs U (female member of the audience)
    ⎡   Ch: Oh, Mr L.–er–I would like er–regarding the, that's the
 1 ⎣   H: We need
    ⎡   H: we certainly need
 2 ⎣   Ch: yes
    ⎡   H: a president or a deputy. Up to now we've gladly had
 3 ⎣   Ch: yes, so it's also
 4   H: Ms A here with us, necessary to have a parents'
 5   representative and it's proved to be
 6   H: yes I er
 7   Ch: very practical when the parents on the committee take
 8   part in the meetings as well because they know about
 9   the issues. Er, do you agree? [names were read out and a
10   vote takes place]
11   Ch: Thank you for taking part in this important election. Er,
12   we now come to the
13   next issue to the /um/ the fixing of the membership fee
</pre>

* * * * *

14 ⎡ U: excuse me, I've got a
   ⎣ Ch: yes
15   U: a question. What's the purpose of the SWC?

It is clear that insufficient information had been made available on the issues that were the subject of the voting, a fact which shows the pro forma nature of the elections.

The same approach to a 'selective' willingness to give information was also evident in the Junior School PA: there was a great willingness to provide information on non-JS PA activities such as school projects and the purchase of equipment. Information concerning the organization of the association itself was limited to the reading out of the names of the candidates who had put themselves forward for election. There was no information as to how or why such decisions had taken place or how one might have been able to participate in them.

Text 18: JS Parents' Association

1	Ch:	So thank you. With this the association's work of the
2		past year has finished–and I would now like to
3		introduce the candidates for election to the Parents'
4		Association election. You've all received a slip of paper.
5		Over the last few days. It was given out in school to
6		your child – that – er – the following people were
7		standing for election for a position on the Parents'
8		Association committee. That's me. I was chairwoman
9		for the previous year [name] and I'm standing for
10		election as chairwoman again for the coming year
11		89/90. The next candidate is Ms K. [Ch reads out the
12		names and explains the voting procedure]
13	Ch:	so – you have the *bottom* – at the bottom of the agenda.
14		Have you all got a slip of paper? Agenda was at the top
15		– then there's a line in the middle and underneath there's
16		the election proposal i.e. the voting slip – underlined on
17		the right-hand side. I would like to ask you to tear off
18		the bottom part or fold it together and: – the people on
19		the slip – with whom you do not agree – whom you
20		don't want – you can cross them out.

The election result which emerges during the meeting after the introductory, formal remarks was hardly surprising:

```
      Ch: chairwoman
       K: Mrs.K., deputy chairwoman
       H: Headmistress
 1    Ch: – right I hear that Ms K's looked at the slips. How many
 2        were there?
 3     K: Thirty-five voting slips and none invalid
 4    Ch: Thirty-five voting slips and none invalid therefore
 5     H: We'd like to congratulate Ms [name CW]
 6    Ch: thank you /applause/ thank you very much
 7     H: and the Parents' Association
```

Important decisions were made, though the parents were not given precise information nor explicitly invited to participate. Criticism, debate and the open questioning of issues were pre-empted and thereby effectively prevented. Selection and manipulation of information thus provide good examples of how hierarchy and power relations in institutions are reinforced: democratic rules and means are neglected, often without those involved even noticing the infractions. Everyone seems eager to participate in the quasi-democratic game.

In Text 19, the GS headmistress is asked for information about the school's PA, and also about the SWC. The headmistress answers selectively, she decides what information should be given and what held back. Thereby, she consciously exercises her power.

Text 19: GS Parents' Association

```
      Ch: chairwoman
       H: headmistress
      Pf: female parent
 1     H: The School
 2    Pf: A question. What does the School Welfare Committee
 3        do?
 4     H: The Welfare Committee consists of three parents, that is
 5        parent parties, so to speak; of three teachers, male and
 6        female; and of three pupils, both male and female, and
 7        they speak about certain issues – for example pupils'
 8        participation in the decision-making process as regards
 9        school regulations. I can't tell you about everything
10        because I can't remember every detail about every rule.
11        We'll certainly be talking about the School Welfare
```

12		Committee in the next meeting, about whether we'll be
13		having a smokers' room or not. – because this matter
14		has already been brought to my attention. There were
15		also a few

16 ⌈ H: other issues
   ⌊ Pf: Oh God /murmurs/

17	H:	that have been brought to my attention. It's the – that
18		are were important for the pupils, that are important for
19		the teachers, that are important for the parents that they
20		discuss there. And if possible, of course, with all the
21		information they can get hold of. The pupil
22		representatives have to hold a meeting beforehand so
23		that they know more or less what their fellow pupils
24		want. The teachers also have a meeting where they
25		discuss what they think is important for them and the
26		parents will hopefully do so too,

27 ⌈ H: think about what they need
   ⌊ Pf: Yes

| 28 | H: | or what they want. Of course, we're often |

29 ⌈ H: confronted with
   ⌊ Ch: Yes

30	H:	problems and then we sit there and just think and
31		sometimes even adjourn the meeting. Sometimes we
32		don't really know what we should be doing there so we
33		go and look for more information. – after all it's a
34		committee, so that all those involved in the school
35		should have a – a certain insight in a certain sense in the
36		decision-making as to what everyday school life should
37		be. – I know – believe me – I know we won't
38		revolutionize the world with it.

In this passage, the headmistress succeeds in presenting a redefinition of the tasks, possibilities and functions of the SWC. She cannot explain everything, because even she cannot remember all the committee's functions and rules, which conflicts with the level of information about the school that a headmistress might be presumed to have. Her appeal for others' trust, her assurances that she only wants the best for everyone and that she can always be relied on, suggest an implicit adoption of a 'mother' role. The elected teacher and student delegates acquiesce to the headmistress's ploy, and seem to consider it not worth trying to come to terms with each individual regulation. In so doing, they effectively relinquish some of their own autonomy. The headmistress mentions an example of the needs of the pupils, the smokers' room, and at the same time defers discussion until the next meeting, indicating that she is well informed about individual requests. In the text, the headmistress repeatedly emphasizes that whatever is important (for pupils, teachers or parents) should be discussed. Such parallelisms have a persuasive and reinforcing function. She then presents her preferred preparation for the SWC – everyone should discuss beforehand in their individual groups – and asks parents to come fully prepared – an implicit and indirect accusation. This interpretation receives immediate confirmation, since – as she says – one cannot discuss something one does not know about in advance. In such a situation, she indirectly threatens to adjourn the meeting.

In the headmistress's opinion, the SWC should provide insights into the everyday life of the schools. Yet this interpretation clearly limits the possibilities for the SWC foreseen in the legislation, which go far beyond merely reporting. Finally, the headmistress concludes with the commonplace 'we [she means the committee here] won't revolutionize the world', to which the chairperson of the PA replies weakly with the equally platitudinous – 'we can have a bit of influence at any rate'. By her apparently objective representation of the committee's function, by giving repeated assurances that there is time and place for everything, while simultaneously defining the (limited) conditions under which the committee is to function, the headmistress succeeds not only in circumscribing the committee's authority, scope and potential, but also in disguising the actual power play this entails.

The next text is an example of the introduction and general presentation of information. As will be seen, the headmistress uses this opportunity for several other functions: positive feedback, strengthening of ingroup, persuasion, etc.

Text 20: SMS school forum

	H	= headmistress
1	H:	what wonderful teachers we have here! And I was actually very pleased, and I
2		passed these on as quickly as possible of course – these reports. That means that

3	people were really very impressed by the classes here –
4	the way in which people get on with each other here –
5	and I have to tell you I know a lot of schools and I too
6	am very impressed. We were all very happy with every
7	class. That there's also something going on – that the
8	children were involved everywhere – that may well
9	cause an odd problem here and there – we're quite
10	aware of that, of course. We've still got a few problems,
11	a few worries with the first-year classes – did I say
12	something wrong? They're still very unruly – and still
13	aren't quite used to the way things run at a secondary
14	modern school – what we expect of them. They've still
15	got a few problems with the discipline, but I think we're
16	hoping that soon enough it'll be all right and we'll soon
17	have them just like in the other classes. And that's also
18	something that I would like to point out as very positive
19	– you notice here that all the teachers pull together.
20	They're all in the same boat together – of course,
21	everyone's free to use his or her methods – but they're
22	all in the same boat. I think that has a really good effect
23	on the atmosphere here. I think that I can really say that
24	– and I really do support it. We recall that a really good
25	experience – when 4C went on their school trip. It was
26	to a wonderful castle – near Radstadt – we saw a video –
27	which Mr. T. made – the class teacher of 4C. He was
28	there with Ms. L. and the children really enjoyed it –
29	had a great time. That was a sporting week – the little
30	angels were everywhere – the weather was excellent –
31	and I haven't heard a single complaint, everyone was
32	really enthusiastic. And I must say that a fourth-year
33	class was able to do this right at the beginning – that it
34	was so successful. We'll be doing more school trips this
35	year – with the first-years and

The president (the headmistress) gave her report at the beginning of the school forum. This report had several functions. First, it was intended as information. Secondly, both teachers and pupils were supposed to consider themselves praised. Thirdly, the importance of this school relative to others was supposed to be evaluated. The fourth and most important function was to challenge all those involved and to produce a strong identification with the institution. So we see that this text has a strong persuasive function, and its 'we' discourse is particularly noticeable. This constitution of solidarity possibly has the additional function of disguising one's own power (placing herself on the same level as the teachers, rather than acknowledging the fact that she has power over them) but could also signify the headmistress's insecurity in the exercise of power.

The headmistress in this example constantly oscillates between distance and identification: 'We're all very happy with every class' is ambiguous in its reference: it could be a kind of *pluralis majestatis* or refer to the school authorities, but certainly does not refer to teachers and pupils involved. 'We recall that a really good experience', on the other hand, clearly indicates the school, the one group available. Later on, those involved were addressed as 'the teachers', and the headmistress spoke in the first person singular, thus signalling the hierarchical distance.

The most important issues in her speech were the opinions of the authorities, the comparison with other schools, the good atmosphere in the school and the school trip as an example of an achievement. Problems were played down ('we still get a few problems') (see lines 7, 9, and 11 of Text 20), and the positive side – i.e. the solidarity and the consensus among the teachers ('they're all in the same boat') – is mentioned immediately. Slogans and clichés follow one another. And the criticism itself becomes weaker, strategically, through the use of a rhetorical question: 'Did I say something wrong?' The text is full of appeals ('but I think we're hoping that soon enough') as well as strong positive norms and attributes (enthusiasm, 'wonderful', etc.). Thus, emotions are addressed and the teachers praised. The headmistress dispatches several issues in a clever way. Criticism is disguised with praise, solidarity and a feeling of community are aroused, and at the same time a break with the hierarchy is achieved: she is informed about everything, pleased with success and impressed with the achievements of the teachers and pupils. If 'everyone is in the same boat', then criticism will not be articulated, and conflicts are made impossible. This indicates another function of the meeting – avoiding open conflict by creating a consensus. Many similarities with the speeches of politicians are suggested. The persuasive function dominates: convincing oneself and everybody else of the superb position and achievements of the school and enlisting everybody in a collective enterprise: a fine example of strategic, institutional thinking.

3.5.4 *Summary*

The detailed analysis of the forms and possibilities of the linguistic realization of the individual steps constituting meetings shows the following result. The linguistic possibilities that are available to chairpersons through legal and statutory regulations and that are, above all, intended to structure the course of meetings, are exploited in many ways so as to influence the content of the meeting and the verbal behaviour of the other participants. This influencing occurs on all relevant levels: on the level of formal procedures, on the level of content, and on the level of direct interaction and specific linguistic formulation.

In the case of emerging conflicts or disagreements, formal measures, such as pointing out the items on the agenda, deferring motions, or terminating meetings, are employed by the chairpersons to avoid such conflicts. By virtue of its formal authority, this behaviour cannot be criticized at all, or only with difficulty.

Content is influenced by the quality of information given when motions are put forward: motions on important subjects such as the election of representatives to school bodies are characterized by a willingness to give only little or selected information on the part of the people putting the motion, most frequently the chairpersons. Pedagogically relevant subjects are presented as decisions that have already been made and need only ratification. Such a transfer of information prevents a concrete discussion of contents in the forum. In the case of less important subjects, such as the decoration of classrooms, information is, of course, adequate and active participation desired. This makes it possible to channel the need for co-determination and cooperation into these 'neutral' areas ('outlet function').

The influencing of the behaviour of participants in meetings by means of linguistic realization of individual steps can be seen in particular in the wording of motions or in the wording of the call to vote. These calls – again especially in the case of important subjects – tend to be formulated in such a way that they contain a clear indication of the desired vote and prevent or impede any other outcome.

In the way they exert influence, all such forms of behaviour are linguistic expressions of power and control by the chairpersons, which leads to passive conduct on the part of the other participants in the meetings. In our analyses this passivity is evinced in a waiver of formal rights, e.g. a vote on an agenda, in a willingness to dispense with adequate and comprehensive information and in a reluctance to ask questions, even when the possibility of doing so is explicitly offered. This lack of readiness to participate increases the scope of 'those in power', who, in a further step, evaluate passive, conflict-avoiding behaviour as something positive. The waiver of formal rights also leads to an ostensible 'debureaucratization' of the course of meetings, along the lines of the slogan 'we don't need any regulations to behave in a democratic way'. Hence this waiver is also a waiver of the necessary possibilities of control to which people are entitled. This creates a vicious circle which can no longer be effectively broken.

This picture is further aggravated by another fundamental feature of the institutional context, as shown in our analyses. In the case of relevant decisions, the democratic, formal and legal conditions can be invalidated by direct interventions and expressions of opinion by the principals by virtue of their supreme position in the hierarchical system of the school, without further need of formal procedures. As the principals always chair school partnership bodies and are always invited to Parents' Association meetings, hierarchical control is always given.

These results make the discrepancies and incompatibilities between the legal regulations on partnership at school and real procedures all too evident. Viewed from the outside, all the necessary or possible formal steps and procedures are fulfilled; true manipulation and exercise of power take place on underlying levels by means of subtle and differentiated verbal strategies. For this reason the concealment of these discrepancies and the true power structures also affects all the levels mentioned. Formally, steps are re- or disfunctionalized to avoid conflict, decisions that have already been made are presented as motions to be discussed, and passivity and unanimity are considered expressions of peaceful harmony, of 'partnership'.

Hence the true functions of school partnership bodies reveal themselves. On the one hand, they represent the formal compliance with legal regulations, e.g. that certain meetings have to take place or that certain subjects and decisions have to be presented to a public consisting of parents and school representatives. On the other, these bodies provide individuals with scope to satisfy their needs for recognition and power.

In my opinion, the reason for the general concealment of the reality of the situation is to be found in the interest of 'those in power' to maintain the status quo (see 1.3 above). This status quo means that real decision-makers hold hierarchically important positions and that is what is crucial is to implement the specific interests of individuals or small groups. In practice there is evidently no concern with transparency, information and active participation.

3.6 Conclusions

The complexity of institutional discourse in schools has been illustrated with several examples. These suggest that gender, power and institutional norms and rules are interwoven in various ways. Using a variety of strategies, powerful persons on committees are able to push their agendas and achieve their preferred results. A very clear order in the vast disorder is established by force (see 1.5.1). These strategies are often disguised in indirect speech acts or discourses, and only through a precise analysis can we uncover the power exercised in such pseudo-democratic institutions. Our main conclusion suggests that democracy cannot be established from above, cannot be institutionalized in a hierarchical domain, such as Austrian schools. As soon as the principals are elected president of the various committees, they transfer their power from one role to the next. Other committee members are dependent, totally or in part, on the principals: pupils are controlled by teachers and principals, while teachers fear for their jobs. In this case, democratization reveals itself as a myth. This brings us back to our discussion of the consequences of greater verbalization and communication in institutions: has the new law changed power structures, or has it led to their mystification? We must draw the conclusion that – in this case – power structures have been reproduced more subtly and have thereby become even more difficult to oppose. The elites have polished their image – they say that they have actually established democracy in schools – but in reality the status quo has been stabilized and legitimized.

Note

1. It is impossible to summarize all the legal details. But it seems important to mention the responsibilities of the various committees:

School Welfare Committee (SWC):

- Consists of elected members from the student body, teachers and parents.
- They make decisions on school projects, political education, career planning programmes, parents' evenings.
- They are consulted on problems about the curriculum and education, as well as about the budget.

Class forum (CF):
- Consists of teacher, student and parent representatives of a class.
- They decide on those class projects which will incur extensive costs; about health care and specific programmes for the class which do not relate to the curriculum.
- They are consulted about the curriculum, education, budget, and other programmes in the school.

School forum (SF):
- Consists of headteacher, all class representatives and main teachers of the grades.
- They make decisions on legal issues affecting the school and on its internal rules.
- They are consulted about the same issues as the CF.

Parents' Association (PA):
- They have participation rights. They are informed about everything that concerns the students, and can take part in teachers' meetings. They can express opinions on the school budget and school materials.
- They also help resolve problems, such as the expulsion of a student.

4 *Understanding the news? Information for the already informed!*

4.1 Introduction

In this chapter, I would like to take a closer look at another kind of institutional discourse, the discourse of the media. Specifically, I will be concerned with radio broadcasts in the Austrian Radio Broadcasting Company (ORF). These are five-minute news bulletins which are broadcast every hour and serve as a major source of information to the Austrian public. In this project (see Lutz/Wodak 1987 for the whole study), we not only described and analysed the discourse, we also studied the comprehensibility and comprehension of the texts by testing Austrian informants of different social backgrounds. The main activity of this project was to reformulate the news in a more comprehensible way and also to test these new versions. Who understood them better and why?[1]

Let us take a short look at the scholarly literature. According to the classic work of Warren (1934), the news should consist of and contain ten elements: actuality, nearness, consequentiality, public importance, drama, curiosity, conflict, sex, emotion and progress. Even though these elements are of different importance in different media, they still cover the entire area of possible news reports.

Unlike drama and fiction, where the texts are, of necessity, self-contained and therefore theoretically inviolable, the news is constructed as an inverted triangle (Wodak *et al.* 1990, Gruber 1991). A news report begins with the most striking item, followed by aspects of lesser importance. The reasons are mainly practical ones – it is easy with this set-up to cut the end off a news item; should the report prove too long, items of lesser importance are dropped. This helps the attentive recipient, too (the same is true for newspapers: the newspaper reader can scan the news faster, headlines provide basic information, with the text that follows elaborating upon them (Lüger 1983)).

Depending on the content of the item, we may identify three types of news story:

fact-stories – individual facts are assembled according to their importance
action (event)-stories – the same action is reported repeatedly but with ever more details
quote-stories – quotations and summaries alternate, the importance decreasing gradually (Warren 1953)[2]

A typical story should contain suspense, highlights, a beginning and an end (Labov/Waletzky 1967). But stories of this structure just do not occur in news bulletins. There is evidence of this text-inherent deficiency at both the macro- and micro-levels. Important units of the kind Sacks has established for narratives, such as interaction units ('today'), justification units ('of course') and recognition type-descriptions ('aha', 'mm') are missing (Sacks 1986). These are units occuring naturally in spoken language, in conversations where backchannels are possible. That is a completely different setting than news in the media.

Imprecise references, pronominalizations, and a lack of feedback are thus also characteristics of these texts (see 4.2.2 below). Typically they are produced unconstrained by a need for self-justification. Consequently, they cannot really be considered stories, as the latter are normally conceived. The relevance of the story is never really explained, background knowledge and hints as to orientation are absent, no frame is available within which to embed the news item. As a result there is almost no possibility of 'updating' it. This situation was confirmed by Larsen, who analysed the intelligibility of Danish news spots (Larsen 1983) (see Wodak/Lutz 1986: 202ff). This suggests that it is often impossible to integrate new information into already available knowledge as long as the present form of providing news items pertains. Little or no acquisition of new knowledge takes place. As Larsen writes:

The main effect of news bulletins apparently is to confirm the

listener's view of the current events, or occasionally, to put new
topics on a mental list of current events. (Larsen 1983: 36)

On the one hand, listening to the news is a process of opinion-
making, where opinions are formed and then – often misunderstood
and unreflected – integrated. Thus stereotypes, clichés and prejudices are confirmed instead of being subjected to critical evaluation
(see 4.6.2 below).

On the other hand, a large part of the population is excluded
altogether from the information provided. To meet its obligations
regarding information and education, the Austrian Broadcasting
Company (ORF) would have to alter the text and the style of
presentation of the news and make it more comprehensible. And
even then we would need tests to see whether simpler news reports
are 'better understood'. As long as news broadcasts retain their
inaccessibility, they will continue to present the large symbolic
capital of the elites. The elites possess information, others are
excluded (van Dijk 1993a). And even if news texts are made more
comprehensible, the elites and better educated profit more from the
greater accessibility (see below). As soon as one considers the
complete news-cycle – from news agency report to newswriter, to
radio reporter or the newspaper that accepts an item, and from
there to the uncomprehending reader – one realizes all the more
clearly what power there is in the passing of news information.

This leads us to our main questions: What do reformulations
mean? What is their impact?

4.2 Project design: language barriers and news

4.2.1 Hypotheses

Our main claim in this project on the discourse of news broadcasts
may be stated as follows: comprehension of news texts is dependent,
on the one hand, on the text itself with respect to form and content
and, on the other, on the cognitive and emotional predisposition of
the listener. Differences in comprehension among listeners are not
necessarily idiosyncratic but can be accounted for by sociological
and socio-psychological factors.

The opposition between *Verstehen* (comprehension) and *Verständlichkeit* (intelligibility) is of great importance. *Verstehen*

applies to the listeners, their environments and motivations, their prior knowledge and listening habits, and thus implies a dynamic process. *Verständlichkeit*, on the other hand, refers to the text, to elements inherent in it (such as morphological and syntactical complexity), and is thus to be understood as a static concept.

The aim of our investigation was to narrow down both aspects, comprehension and comprehensibility, the listener and the text, and to provide some answers to the central questions: How do different people understand different texts and why? Who understands what?

4.2.2 Procedure and methods

Two independent investigations were carried out. In the first, pupils produced written versions of recorded news bulletins (13 classes from various schools types were used, 277 subjects altogether). In the second investigation, oral recall tests and interviews were made (see below 4.5.1).

The news was presented in three different versions: the original form and two 'simplified', reformulated versions. The second (alternative) reformulation was simpler than the first, and was augmented by headlines and read by alternating speakers. Special emphasis was laid on shortening long and complex sentences, as well as on the expansion of nominal phrases and the explicit highlighting of contextual relationships or contradictions within a given news item – in short, on a general increase in the semantic coherence of individual stories. It was consequently possible to test empirically, for the first time on such a large scale, previous tentative hypotheses about making the news intelligible, on the basis of reproduction performance. The pupils produced written versions of all three versions of each news bulletin.

The selection of the news texts posed a problem: it was important that they contain original and up-to-date news to maintain credibility (Larsen 1983), but we also wanted to use the same texts for a large number of test-persons and the texts also had to be reformulated, which again took time. We solved the problem by choosing original news reports which, though not actually up-to-date, could have been. What they did contain was **latent topicality**. The choice of such texts was not without its problems though, since reality might possibly 'overtake' latent topical events (wars might break out or re-erupt under new circumstances, ministers could resign, etc.). Luckily this did not happen to our texts (Text I [Sauha] from 5 January 1984, 11 p.m.; Text II [Lebanon] from 30 September 1984, 3 p.m.; and Text III [Flick] from 28 December 1983, 2 p.m.). The empirical investigation took place at the beginning of 1985, at which time political events had not upset the logical consistency of our texts.

The news texts chosen were of about equal length. They were taken from the hourly short news broadcasts of the '3rd programme' (Ö-3), the weather report was eliminated (for obvious reasons), so the actual length of the three broadcasts was approximately four minutes.

The use of 'not really topical' news does, admittedly, pose a problem, in so far as the real 'updating process' cannot function in its normal way. It is not possible to proceed on the basis of up-to-the-minute daily knowledge; one has to rely on general prior knowledge of political processes.

Despite these problems, 'latent topicality' worked excellently for our experiment. Not one of the 277 test-persons was surprised by the news content, and most did not even notice the lack of topicality. One example:

'Sauha Austria I'[3]

The situation in the Alberner Hafen [harbour] area of Vienna, where conservationists are seeking to prevent the clearing of the water-meadows in the so-called Sauhaufen, has come to a head today. In the early morning and with police protection about 50 workmen with 4 shovel dredgers started a large-scale clearing operation. A group of conservationists is attempting to prevent them. They have lain down on the ground in front of trucks and have climbed up trees. The police have arrested a number of people. The whole Sauhaufen area has been sealed off by police. The Vienna Harbour Company is claiming the area as dump for a rubble. [my translation]

'Sauha Österreich I'

Die Situation im Gebiet des Alberner Hafens in Wien, wo Umweltschützer die Rodung des Auwaldes im sogenannten Sauhaufen verhindern wollen, hat sich heute zugespitzt. Am frühen Morgen haben etwa 50 Arbeiter mit 4 Schaufelbaggern unter dem Schutz der Polizei mit einer großangelegten Holzschlägerungsaktion begonnen.

Eine Gruppe von Umweltschützern versucht sie daran zu hindern. Sie haben sich vor die Lastfahrzeuge gelegt und sind auf Bäume geklettert. Die Polizei hat mehrere Personen festgenommen. Das gesamte Gebiet des Sauhaufens ist von Polizisten abgeriegelt. Die Wiener Hafengesellschaft beansprucht das Gebiet als Schüttgutdeponie.

'Sauha Austria (reformulation 1)'

In the Alberner Hafen in Vienna conservationists are seeking to prevent the clearing of the watermeadows in the so-called Sauhaufen. The situation has come to a head today. In the early morning and with police protection about 50 workmen with 4 shovel dredgers started to clear the forest. The conservationists have lain down on the ground in front of trucks and have climbed up trees. The police have arrested a number of people. The whole Sauhaufen area has been sealed off by police. The Vienna Harbour Company is claiming the area as a dump for rubble. [my translation]

Sauha Österreich (reformulation 1)

Beim Alberner Hafen in Wien wollen Umweltschützer die Rodung des Auwaldes im sogenannten Sauhaufen verhindern. Die Situation hat sich heute zugespitzt. Am frühen Morgen haben etwa 50 Arbeiter mit 4 Schaufelbaggern unter dem Schutz der Polizei mit der Rodung des Waldes begonnen. Die Umweltschützer haben sich vor Lastfahrzeuge gelegt und sind auf Bäume geklettert. Die Polizei hat mehrere Personen festgenommen. Das gesamte Gebiet des Sauhaufens ist von Polizisten abgeriegelt. Die Wiener Hafengesellschaft beansprucht nämlich das Gebiet als Schüttgutdeponie.

'Sauha Austria (reformulation 2)'

In the Alberner Hafen in Vienna, the district of Simmering, clashes are occurring between conservationists and the police. In the early morning about 50 workmen with police protection started clearing the watermeadows because the Vienna Harbour Company is claiming the area as a dump for rubble. The conservationists laid down on the ground in front of trucks and climbed up trees to prevent the felling. The police have arrested a number of demonstrators and sealed off the whole so-called Sauhaufen area. [my translation]

Sauha Österreich (reformulation 2)

*In Wien Simmering kommt es beim Alberner Hafen zu Ausschrei-
tungen zwischen Umweltschützern und der Polizei. Am frühen
Morgen begannen etwa 50 Arbeiter unter Polizeischutz mit der
Rodung des Auwaldes, weil die Wiener Hafengesellschaft das Gebiet
als Schüttdeponie beansprucht. Die Umweltschützer legten sich vor
Lastautos und kletterten auf Bäume, um die Rodung zu verhindern.
Die Polizei hat mehrere Demonstranten festgenommen und das
gesamte Gebiet des sogenannten Sauhaufens abgeriegelt.*

In order to be able to integrate emotional and motivational aspects,
media-related behaviour, and complex socio-psychological parameters, all of which present particular problems in evaluation, we
decided to carry out interviews with subjects selected according to
social class, age and gender. Altogether, we did 50 in-depth
interviews of about one hour each with randomly selected subjects
of different social backgrounds.

The points of discussion in the interviews were related to
listeners' attitudes and media-related behaviour: i.e. to the reasons
for their reliance on the media, their attitudes towards the intelligibility and language of news broadcasts; the informativeness and
objectivity of the reports; the degree of their emotional involvement
and level of interest; their suggestions for a reorganization of news
programming, etc. In addition, we carried out several psycholinguistic tests, in order to approach the comprehension phenomenon
from the greatest possible number of angles. In these the subjects
reproduced recorded news bulletins orally, summarized other news
items, defined certain lexical terms, filled out cloze tests, etc. (see
Lutz/Wodak 1987).

4.3 Digression: What do we mean by 'comprehension' and 'understanding'?

Before I actually present some of the most important results, I
would like to discuss the major theoretical issues involved.

The psychologist Hans Hörmann once formulated very precisely
the difficulties in understanding 'understanding,' or, to put it more
accurately, *Verstehen*:

> Understanding [*Verstehen*] is a concept about which we would like
> to say, initially and tentatively, that it concerns communication

procedures in the broadest sense of the term. It is a word which we all use every day; many of us use it in scholarly publications as well. Educationalists, historians, political scientists, psychiatrists, and philologists all speak of understanding, but there is no one accepted definition or even a definition which is used predominantly in any one of these disciplines, much less a definition which transcends them. The explanations which accompany this concept, or which one must make for oneself, are, it is said, as varied and divergent as the interpretations of the smile of Mona Lisa. (Hörmann 1983: 13)

My own countless forays into the linguistic, socio-psychological and psychological literature have still not led me to even a usable definition of *Verstehen*, much less a theory that could really explain 'understanding' and 'misunderstanding' in actual written and oral communication. The problem begins with the translation of *Verstehen* into English, for the precise boundaries between understanding and comprehension are not always clear, though clearly comprehension (or intelligibility) is more cognitively connoted and hence more circumscribed in its usages than understanding. We are forced to tread lightly, for there are too many interconnected factors and varieties of approach to the problem. For example, there is the traditional hermeneutics of Schleiermacher, the interpretation of theological texts, the epistemological dispute over explanation (*Erklären*) and understanding (*Verstehen*) (Wittgenstein 1967, etc.), or the concept as it is used in psychoanalysis, broadly defined (cf. Freud 1976, Habermas 1971, 1969; cf. the discussion in Lutz/ Wodak 1987, Lutz 1988, Antos/Augst 1989, Scherner 1989, Maas 1988). I shall return to this discussion later.

In everday speech, we encounter many meanings und usages of the word *Verstehen*, which can include both understanding and comprehension: the possible meanings range from acoustic possibilities ('I cannot understand anything here because it is so loud') to an identification with another person (empathy) which is emotional and interactive ('I understand how you feel'). The German expression *Wir verstehen einander gut* captures these relational, emotional and cognitive aspects of 'understanding well' (in English one would say 'We get along well'). Moreover, how could understanding ever be verified? Is the mere taking notice of what is being said understanding? Is simulation, reproduction, memorizing or the solving of problems (action) understanding? We will return to this, when presenting empirical results from our socio-psycholinguistic study on 'text comprehension'. In my view, this difficult concept can be properly grasped and operationalized only by employing methods and data from many different sources (see 1.4 above).

When we study text comprehension, we have to deal with many questions and unresolved problems:

How does comprehension (*Verstehen*) differ from comprehensibility (*Verständlichkeit*)?
How does text comprehension (*Textverstehen*) differ from text production (*Textproduktion*)?
How does the understanding of a text (*Textverstehen*) differ from the interpretation of a text (*Textinterpretation*)?
Does the type of text play a role, and, if so, what?
Do coherence and context play a role, and, if so, what?
How does one 'understand' these distinctions?

Before offering a few tentative answers to these questions, it would be worthwhile discussing the differing traditions of *Verstehen*. 'The task [of hermeneutics]', argues Schleiermacher, 'can also be expressed as understanding the speech act. For while we have no direct knowledge of what goes on inside [the speaker's mind], we must make explicit many things, which can remain unconscious to him' (Schleiermacher 1977: 94). For Schleiermacher, understanding and explaining are not in conflict: explaining is as integral a part of understanding as the 'psychological interpretation'. The interpreter, in Schleiermacher's framework, understands more than the author, even transcends the text and recognizes the motives of the speaker (or writer) and is able to proffer explanations. And thus we come to Freudian psychoanalysis, which as theory and metatheory is concerned with uncovering the unconscious, that is with making the unconscious conscious. Freud argued:

When I postulate the interest of the language scholar in psycho-analysis, I certainly overstep the [limits of the] customary meaning of words. Language must not be understood simply as the expression of ideas in words, but also as sign (body) language and every type of expression of psychic activity, as well as the written word. Then, however, it is legitimate to argue that the interpretations of psycho-analysis are above all translations from a means of expression that is foreign to us into one more familiar to our thought processes. (Freud, *Gesammelte Werke*, Vol. XV, 1976: 62) [my translation]

In the first case, the 'traditional hermeneutics' of Schleiermacher, it is a question of a skill (which one can acquire – Schleiermacher does provide a methodology); in the second, understanding is an integral component of the psychoanalytic method, that is, of the establishment of transference and of the technique of interpretation. In this second sense, understanding becomes in the final analysis an act of either an intrapsychic or a social kind. Neither Schleiermacher nor Freud, however, offers a systematic theory or model, nor does either suggest a methodology or heuristic aids to this meaning.

This failing has come under renewed and justified criticism in the cognitive sciences, which have been searching for an explicit description and explanation of the process of understanding (*Verstehensvorgang*) ('Explanations must also be understood!', Schmidt 1973: 7; Scherner 1989). Moreover, other psychologists and adherents of cognitive science have sought a metatheory both of scientific and everyday cognition and of action in general. A systematic concept of understanding would offer the basis for such a metatheory. Thus conceived, understanding would be defined above all by an integration of new facts into pre-existing knowledge and different types of knowledge (*Wissenswelt*) (e.g. Tulving 1972), albeit within pre-existing frames and schemata (see below; Wodak 1986a, 1992). Until now the socio-psychological dimension, co- and con-text have been excluded from this definition. Restricting the definition of understanding to small and even the smallest of samples (which would correspond to ethnomethodology and conversational analysis: see Cicourel 1987; Brown/Yule 1985, etc.) and to the cognitive dimension alone (thus neglecting the whole problem of context, emotions and society) (see van Dijk 1989, Wodak 1989) destines such attempts to failure.

In interaction and communication in everyday life, we know, however, that conflicts, inequality and misunderstanding, thus **disorders**, are the rule rather than the exception. Social actions are never completely rational or clear-cut: they are overdetermined, ambivalent and multi-layered, with both cognitive and emotional moments. This recommends again, as demonstrated above, an interdisciplinary discourse sociolinguistic approach, which can incorporate such considerations.

4.4 Critical linguistics and an interpretative theory of *Verstehen*

Discourse sociolinguistics, therefore, poses the questions of under-standing or comprehension and misunderstanding in a general manner: who understands or does not understand what, why, where and with what effects? What does this signify socially and politi-cally? Finally, one must ask what the 'optimization' of texts (*Textoptimierung*), that is, their reformulation in a more compre-hensible language, means and whom it benefits? Are disorders in discourse really eliminated, or do new and different ones merely take the place of the old? This question takes us back to the central question throughout this book: are changes in and through lan-guage emancipatory and helpful, or do they serve better to disguise injustice (see 1.6 above)? We may come closer to an answer to this fundamental question by investigating processes of understanding.

4.4.1 The concept of the schema

In the discussion that follows, I employ the word 'schema' as the most general cognitive concept, forming a continuum with the concepts 'frame' and 'script' (see Lutz 1988: 77 for a detailed discussion and literature). In this I follow above all the tradition of Bartlett (Bartlett 1932). The basic idea of all concepts which work with global models is a simple one: to represent interconnections by means of schemata. In one schema, these interconnections represent cultural, historical and other experiences. Through the employment of the 'accident'-schema, for example, when I read about an automobile accident in the newspaper, I am able to draw inferences that transcend the explicit information provided. Thus, I would be tempted to ask whether the driver was driving too fast, if he or she had been drinking or if it was dark or misty. I would go on by asking how many people were killed or wounded, how extensive the damage was, and who had been guilty. Did the police appear on the scene, were more than two cars involved? This is, by the way, an essential point in the construction of prejudice and of judgements in general.

Understanding is in this sense schema-oriented: (on the concept of cognitive schema see Schank/Abelson 1977, Minsky 1980, Ballstaedt *et al.* 1981a,b). That is, comprehension does not function on the basis of a *tabula rasa* in the human mind, but is to a large extent dependent on schematic prior knowledge. I do not want to elaborate the 'integrative model of text comprehension' in detail (see Lutz/Wodak 1987, Wodak 1992), but shall focus on the socio-cognitive approach, by distinguishing three types of 'schema' which guide our process of understanding and thus have a critical impact on the design of our study.

4.4.1.1 *Cognitive schemata*

On the basis of their prior knowledge, listeners are capable of extending the propositional content of the message above and beyond the information provided by the news text, as well as elaborating on this content, drawing inferences, and recognizing the intentions of the individuals and groups involved. The more structured the schema, the easier it is to understand the text.

For the reception of a news text, this implies that only when a conceptual framework for a particular context is present in a given individual is he or she in a position to be 'informed' by the news item. For example, when a person has missed out on the latest developments in national politics while on holiday, it is difficult to understand the news on their return. Put another way, how can one understand news about Central America or the Middle East if one has no knowledge of these countries? The only possibility for uninformed listeners is to (re-)activate their own prejudices, as we observed with several of our interview partners.

4.4.1.2 *Formal schemata*

Through socialization processes and later experience, listeners are intuitively acquainted with particular text types and their conventional forms. Thus, they have a knowledge of the degree to which texts of a given type are normally structured (in so far as they are familiar with this text type), and of the points in a given text where one can expect to meet particular elements of semantic content. If a given text conforms to the listener's expectations with respect to structure, then the processing of information will be facilitated.

For the reception of news texts, this implies that listeners are well acquainted with the structure of news broadcasts. For example, headlines, the time announcement, and the weather report are expected at specific points in the broadcast. Within the individual news story, characterized by a recognizable 'headline style', the listener expects a summary of the contents in the first sentence of the story, which is in fact most often the case. For the same reason (summarizing of the story at the beginning and not at the end), it is often not possible to reconstruct the semantic coherence of a news item if one misses the first sentence.

4.4.1.3 Emotional schemata

Listeners – conditioned by socialization processes, profession, age, gender, etc. – are thus placed in a unique position. They have interests, goals, opinions, needs and ideas concerning norms and values, and individual attitudes to a given text, flexible to varying degrees, have an effect on comprehension (van Dijk 1980: 129ff): the more relevant a text proves to be for a given listener, the more intensively it will be processed, and the better it will be retained in the memory.

Comprehension of news texts is also dependent on the emotional distance on the part of the listener. The more emotional (positive or negative) the reaction evoked by the news item, the better the comprehension and retention of the material presented.

4.4.2 The concept of strategy

It was the approach of van Dijk and Kintsch (1983) that first made it possible to effect an extensive conceptual separation of the term 'strategy' from related terms such as 'rule', 'plan', 'tactic', 'heuristic', etc. Van Dijk and Kintsch define strategy as follows:

> Intuitively, a strategy is the idea of an agent about the best way to act in order to reach a goal. For our purpose we will, indeed, take a strategy to be a cognitive representation of some kind, just as a plan was defined as a cognitive representation of some macroaction. Now, whereas a plan is a global concept of the macroaction and its final result or goal, a strategy is a global representation of the means of reaching that goal. This overall means will dominate a number of lower level, more detailed, decisions and actions ... Note the difference between a plan and a strategy. A plan is merely a global representation of an action, for example, 'Taking a plane to New York'. A strategy, however, is a global mental representation of a

style, that is, of a way of doing this global action in the most effective way (e.g. with low cost, minimum risk, etc.) (van Dijk/Kintsch 1983: 64f)

Strategies thus correspond fairly closely to our intuitive under-standing of how text comprehension (and also text planning) takes place. The interplay of strategies, rules and schemata is particularly useful in explaining the comprehension process, as strategies alone are too powerful. In text comprehension, strategies cannot function as an endless selection process, but must be 'channelled' by comparatively rigid rules. On top of this, there also exist cultural and subcultural experience patterns of cognitive schemata, which control the specific selection of strategies.

4.4.3 *The integrative model of comprehension*

On the basis of these brief, and necessarily compressed, definitions and guiding assumptions, I would like to turn to an initial model of comprehension which attempts to incorporate and thereby solve the problems of text and context as well as of the interacting agents. With this model (or heurisma) we can transcend the purely cognitive approach.

The model of socio-psychological text planning (cf. Wodak 1986) cannot, of course, simply be reversed in order to describe the process of text comprehension. However, we can postulate that important, empirically tested, variables (age, class, education, profession, gender, culture, previous knowledge, personality, tex-tual experience) also play a role in text comprehension.

This means that a listener or reader initially attempts to assign what he or she hears or reads to a frame, that certain strategies scan the original text in order finally to obtain the textual basis (the meaning, plan, the subject). On the other hand, this process is dependent on socio-psychological parameters, including the actual situation.

The constitutive features may be summarized as follows:

- Our model is a constructional one, i.e. the listener/reader constructs a representation that is not an exact copy of the text in his or her memory, and we suppose that there is no one textual basis common to all listeners/readers (cf. however van Dijk/Kintsch 1983).

- Discrepancies arise from the fact that in a given context social factors interact with cognitive ones. That is, the listener/reader constructs, in addition to the simple representation of the text, a representation of the social context, and these representations interact with one another (cf. the double representation model in van Dijk/Kintsch 1983: 338ff.).
- Comprehension is a cyclical process. This is valid for the interaction between text and context (socio-psychological influences) as well as for top-down and bottom-up cognitive processes ('depth' of comprehension).
- Our model is an interpretative one: the listener/reader interprets the text, he or she hears and constructs a meaning out of it (cf. Hörmann 1983: 506).

4.4.4 The cyclical comprehension process

The starting point of text comprehension is, on the one hand, the text presentation (e.g. legal text, news broadcast) and, on the other, the reader/listener with her or his individual social, socio-psychological and psychological characteristics, formed by prior knowledge of and emotional attitudes to the institution and its products (see Figure 4.1). The predisposition of each reader/listener is defined in the light of their individual schema-oriented prior knowledge, with regard to contextual, cognitive associations, knowledge of the formal structure of the text genre news and emotional attitude towards the information transmitted through the news and its significance to the individual's own life-style. These three different areas of schemata can vary widely for the individual listener and thus represent the preconditions for differences in text comprehension. Individual schemata that strategically control text comprehension are activated in the test subject by the text presentation. The more marked a certain contextual, cognitive schema in a reader/listener, the more precisely and explicitly can further text processing be controlled. The cognitive schemata activated by the reader/listener now control further text comprehension in combination with top-down and bottom-up cognitive processes ('bottom-up' processes are text-oriented, 'top-down' processes are directly or indirectly schema-oriented). Both top-down and bottom-up cognitive processes and the activation of the schema are not linear but cyclical. Further sub-

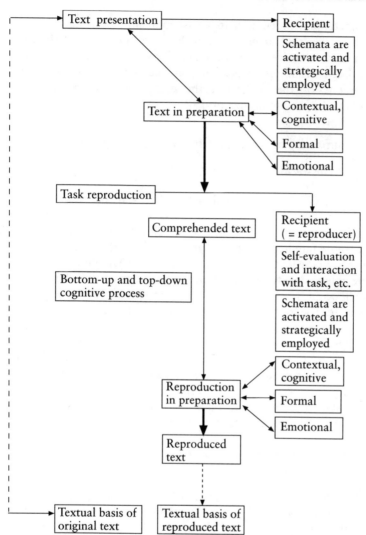

Figure 4.1: The 'Integrative Comprehension Model'

schemata can be activated by the text in addition to those schemata previously activated; on the other hand, text assimilation operators can be controlled by schemata. The 'text in preparation' expresses this dimension of the comprehension process: the text which is being comprehended at that precise moment at various levels. As soon as the 'text in preparation' has been processed sufficiently long and intensively by the reader/listener (= 'depth of understanding', which is dependent on the attitude, interests and intentions of the recipient), the comprehended text becomes available (in long-term memory).

4.5 Summary of some significant quantitative results

4.5.1 *News-recall*

The news discourse was analysed qualitatively and quantitatively on the basis of text-linguistic and psycholinguistic methods. In both investigations the results were quite clear: middle-class subjects were more familiar with the language used in news broadcasts than those from the lower-middle and lower class.[4] Middle-class subjects were able to deal with this language significantly better than lower-middle- and working-class subjects, receptively as well as productively. The 'social class' factor had a significant influence on the test results in almost all of the tests carried out; the 'gender' factor was significant as well. However, an interlacing of the variables was often to be observed (e.g. gender and social class). In addition, factors such as the topic of a given news item, the listener's interest in and prior knowledge of that topic, as well as the degree of their political involvement, contributed considerably to the test results.

Here are some examples from the recall test:

5.00 p.m. news, 28 December 1983 (original text)
West Germany

There has been a new development in the affair concerning the West German company Flick. The government in Bonn has issued a decree to the concern according to which Flick is to pay back a tax rebate of about 3.2 billion Austrian shillings which is connected with the so-called party donations affair and the charge levelled against the Minister for Economic Affairs, Otto Graf Lambsdorff. A tax exemption status had been granted to the concern for investing in the American conglomerate Grace. Government spokesman Bönisch declared that the prerequisite for such a dispensation, which had been assumed when the exemption was issued, had never existed. Shortly after the announcement, Flick instituted legal proceedings at the competent Administrative Court in Cologne. Minister for Economic Affairs Lambsdorff is accused of having accepted party donations from Flick and, in return, of having supported its tax exemption status in the cabinet.

How did the subjects recall this item?

> A: Could you retell as exactly as possible what – eh – what was just said? What was it all about?
>
> B: Well, that Graf Lambsdorff, that he was bribed by Flick. And – eh – took money. And the like. And – eh – now that is – eh – eh – Flick wants to – refuses to. That it made – eh – these donations. But they have gone into the matter.
>
> A: Mhm – any details? Can you remember any?
>
> B: Well, I didn't really look out for details. Let's say just the most important things.
>
> (Example 10; Interview 35:6)

This reproduction can be termed 'average'. The following summary is much more detailed and closer to the text:

> A: Mhm – could you retell the report as precisely as possible? What was it all about?
>
> B: Yes – it reports – that Flick – tried – eh – to save taxes by – eh – bribing – eh – politicians by financing a party. Eh – it was about 3.2 billion shillings. Which – eh – which were to be saved by Flick investing in the American company Grace. Ah – Graf Lambsdorff was accused. That he supported Flick in the government. – And –
>
> A: Any other details?
>
> B: Mhm – yes – that proceedings were instituted at the Administrative Court.
>
> (Example 11; Interview 37:4)

In this summary almost all the crucial information is reproduced, an exceptionally high reproduction performance compared with the average. Yet a 'summary' can look completely different:

> A: Could you retell the report as exactly as possible? What was it all about?
>
> B: Yes – we've read and heard this and that. All about them up there – the big fish – then you remember.
>
> A: Well – what was it all about?
>
> B: Ah – parties and money – donations by – (..........)
>
> A: And who did what?

B: Well, Flick – somehow, like – probably embezzled its donation money or something like that.

A: Mhm – mhm.

B: I don't listen so exact. (...........) You can't do anything about it anyway.

(Example 12; Interview 31:5)

Here only two elements of the news item were reproduced. What is particularly striking is that the respondent (resignedly) incorporates the report into his own world view, 'the big fish', 'You can't do anything about it anyway'. On being asked to retell the report he has heard, he presents his own attitude; the report only forms the background to his own opinion. After the summaries we asked the informants if they had followed these events in the media, which most of them affirmed (81.6% yes, 18.4% no), even if they had supplied a poor summary.

The recall test was done twice, immediately after the news item was played, and at the end of the interview.

Now to the results. We summarized the reproductive perform-ance in sums (one point per crucial news element: SUM A, immediately following the broadcast, SUM B, at the end of the interviews). For example, for SUM A: Example 10, three points, Example 11, eight points and Example 12, two points (see above). A classification according to gender and class showed differences, age-specific differences were not seen (Tables 4.1 and 4.2).

Class-specific differences make themselves manifest in a con-tinuous growth in reproductive performance, from the working class (2.8 and 1.6 points) (SUM A and SUM B) over the lower-middle class (3.7 and 3.0 points) to the middle class (4.52 and 3.8 points), so the class-specific differences established in the summaries

Table 4.1: Gender-, class- and age-specific differences in the summary test, at the beginning of the interview. Comparison of sums.

	Gender			Social class			Age		
	m	f	WC	LMC	MC	–25	26–45	45–
SUM A	4.52	3.52	2.80	3.70	4.52	4.00	5.05	4.00
Mean								
Significance	$(\alpha = 0.0637)$			4.02 $(\alpha = 0.1150)$			–		

WC = working class; LMC = lower-middle class; MC = middle class.

Table 4.2: Gender-, class- and age-specific differences in the summary test, at the end of the interview. Comparison of sums.

	Gender			Social class			Age		
	m	f	WC	LMC	MC	–25	26–45	45–
SUM B	3.76	2.76	1.60	3.00	3.80	3.05	3.37	3.45
Mean				3.26				
Significance	(α = 0.0657)			(α = 0.0452)			–	

WC = working class; LMC = lower-middle class; MC = middle class.

can also be seen! The overall average (4.02 and 3.26 points) is exceptionally small (a total of 10 points could in principle be achieved): the informants could not reproduce the report completely (this also applies to most of the educated members of the middle class), many elements of substance simply 'disappear', even on concentrated listening. So the comprehension barrier affects everybody, not just certain underprivileged groups. In accordance with our assumptions for the test, at the end of the interviews significantly fewer news elements were reproduced than immediately after listening. The overall average was 4.02 (immediately afterwards) as opposed to 3.26 (half an hour later). So short-term memory also plays a major role in reproductive performance, as many cognitive-psychological tests have demonstrated (cf. Wessels 1984).

What about the formal side of the summaries? As mentioned above, here we established that formal deviations from the situation of summarizing occurred when respondents made global assertions about politicians and politics. Gender and age-specific differences were not seen, but there were highly significant class-specific ones: the working class and (partly also) the lower-middle class make global assertions much more frequently than the middle class. Only the middle class appears able to adapt to the formal demands of a summary; the working class and the lower-middle class tend rather to take a stance immediately, to introduce their point of view. Such behaviour is considerably 'more natural' than just summarizing the news without comment, for these are the obvious reactions in 'normal' consumption of the news. We interpret these differences as follows. Only the educated person, who has learnt in years of socialization at school to abstract from concrete facts, can succeed in producing an 'oversophisticated' summary that does not conform to the 'natural' mode of retelling and commenting. So in the case of oral retelling we can see the formal differences in reproduction between social groups, which do not occur in written summary because of the restrictive situation. Oral retelling gives the informants much more scope for 'personal' presentation (which is, however, of a systematic nature) than the taught and restrictive situation of written summary.

4.5.2 Written summaries

The Austrian secondary school system comprises 'high schools' (*Mittelschulen*, academically oriented schools leading to university entrance) and vocational schools of various types (*Berufsschulen*, where apprentices attend classes one day a week). The choice of school is dependent almost without exception on social class. Between these types of school we observed highly significant differences in the amount of material reproduced: the high-school students mentioned significantly more individual news items and their summaries were at least 50% longer than those of the apprentices. Among the high-school students the girls produced better results; among the apprentices the boys. See Table 4.3. Again, I would like to present some examples of written summaries. The code numbers stand for the persons tested. The original news item was SAUHA (see above).

C10 (code numbers)
Clashes between conservationists (Hainburg) and police, a number of demonstrators, who had climbed onto trees to prevent the felling, arrested, 100 workmen demonstrated in favour of Hainburg, the police sealed off the area.

C36
In Linz and Vienna there were clashes between conservationists and the police. Unfortunately, the latter had to intervene when the conservationists illegally prevented work in the Sauhaufen area.

B02
Sauhaufen occupied by conservationists because it is to be cleared, cordoned off by police, arrests already made, 50 workmen with 4 bulldozers – conservationists lie down in front of bulldozers, area is to serve as a rubble dump.

Table 4.3: Average length of summaries for each news item/school type/gender (measured in number of words).

	Summary 1		Summary 2		Summary 3		Weighted average of sum. 1–sum. 3	
	f	m	f	m	f	m	f	m
High-school students	11.77 (65)	9.95 (93)	10.88 (66)	8.99 (95)	14.51 (66)	13.22 (95)	12.39 (197)	10.73 (283)
Apprentices	4.80 (60)	5.24 (48)	4.60 (59)	5.35 (48)	6.06 (59)	7.74 (49)	5.15 (178)	6.12 (145)
Overall average (weighted)	8.43 (125)	8.35 (141)	7.91 (125)	7.77 (143)	10.52 (125)	11.35 (144)	8.95 (375)	9.17 (428)

B16
Conservationists oppose the clearing of the so-called 'Sauhaufen', with police protection 4 workmen with bulldozers began clearing work, conservationists climbed onto trees and lay down in front of machines.

4.5.3 Reformulations

Let us take another example of a news item in both its original form and reformulations.

LEBANON Middle East

Early today the Israeli air force again attacked targets in Lebanon. They bombed positions of the pro-Iranian Shiite militia in the north of the Syrian-controlled Bekaa Valley and in the vicinity of the historical town of Baalbek. Radio Beirut reports 60 dead and 300 injured. The Syrians speak of at least 17 dead and 106 injured as well as a large number of people missing. An Israeli military spokesman declared all aircraft had returned to their bases undamaged. It was the ninth Israeli air raid since the bomb attack on the headquarters of the Israeli occupation forces in the southern Lebanese town of Sidon.

LEBANON Middle East (reformulation 1)

Early today the Israeli air force again attacked targets in Lebanon. It was the ninth Israeli air raid in Lebanon since the bomb attack on the headquarters of the Israeli occupation forces in the southern

Lebanese town of Sidon. The Israelis bombed positions of the pro-Iranian Shiite militia in the north of the Syrian-controlled Bekaa Valley and in the vicinity of the historical town of Baalbek. Lebanese radio reports 60 dead and 300 injured. On the other hand, the Syrians speak of at least 17 dead and 106 injured as well as a large number of missing. An Israeli military spokesman declared all aircraft had returned to their bases undamaged.

LEBANON Middle East (reformulation 2)

In Lebanon there are again armed clashes. Early today the Israeli air force once more attacked positions of the pro-Iranian Shiite militia. The north of the Syrian-controlled Bekaa Valley and the vicinity of the historical town of Baalbek were the scenes of the clashes. State-run Lebanese radio reports 60 dead and 300 injured. On the other hand, the Syrians speak of only 17 dead and 106 injured as well as a large number of missing.

The reformulations were spoken on to tape by 'original' ORF speakers in the studio, so as to retain the semblance of authenticity. We found this of great importance as such a procedure preserved the ritual of 'radio news' in significant respects (the outer framework and the recognized voice of the speaker), so the surprise effect (distorting reception) described above was largely avoided (see 4.2.2). We can summarize these reformulations as follows. The type of text was not basically altered, and we placed emphasis on producing the greatest coherence and cohesion. This was expressed in the addition of content, omission of details and addition of conjunctions and linking half-sentences. The third one was the most coherent and explicit, by way of argumentation and elaboration of the topic.

What were the results? The reformulated versions (simplifications) of the news produced the desired effect: subjects were able to reproduce more material in the written summaries than after the original presentation; the increase was however significantly greater among high-school students than apprentices (see Figure 4.2).

These results were not quite what we expected and, for other reasons, actually somewhat discouraging. On the one hand, it was possible to improve comprehension with reformulation; on the other hand, those who understood less anyway profited less from the reformulation. *The social gap in fact widened* and discrepancies between social groups became even more significant! Thus,

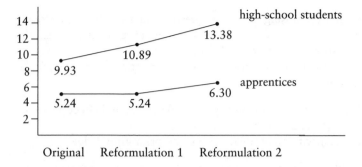

Figure 4.2: Effects of the Reformulations

language reform, in this case, helped the elites, not the excluded others. This means that emancipation and reform cannot be effected on the basis of language only; indeed, only large structural change in society as a whole would allow the inclusion of the excluded.

4.6 The limits of quantification – qualitative analysis of some interview texts

4.6.1 Introduction

In this section I would like to illustrate – using transcribed replies from the interviews[5] – a number of outstanding problem areas. This should give an indication of the diversity of opinions and attitudes that emerged from the interviews, a diversity which, eventually, had to be pared down to allow for the dichotomous categories necessary for quantitative interpretation. It is not possible here to present a complete discourse-analytical investigation; that lies beyond the scope of this specific research. Since the interviews were a means to an end, they served to gain access to background data on the interviewees, probing attitudes and prior knowledge. The interview texts were not the 'real object' of the investigation (see Wodak 1987a, Lutz 1988 for details). However, not only does the qualitative interview-analysis offer an illustration, it also has theoretical and methodological value, and could potentially serve a 'metafunction': to reflect on one's own procedure (with the collection of data, the encoding and the interpretation) (Lutz 1988), because we are aware that the posing of certain questions in a specific way already has implications for the possible range of answers. Thus, the answers should not be viewed out of context.

Two critical points that illustrate the limitations of pure quantification are:

(a) listening habits (is listening to the news the main occupation or just incidental to some other task?)
(b) the ability to integrate the news into prior knowledge.

Thus, what formal, cognitive and emotional comprehension schemata are used, what micro- and macro-strategies? I would argue that listening and updating largely have to do with emotional factors – attitudes, motivation, interests, prior knowledge, prejudices, etc. First, upon hearing the news the interviewees immediately classified the information according to normative categories, e.g. right or wrong, good or bad, etc.; or, secondly, they reacted indifferently to the news, it had no obvious direct bearing on their lives, as will be shown immediately.

4.6.2 *The ability to integrate news into background knowledge*

In this part of the interview we tried to find a method to compare the test person's self-assessment with her or his real ability to reproduce certain news items. Questions focused mainly on news about the Lebanon. We wanted to know about its integration into the informant's background knowledge and about their assessment of it. We were particularly interested in finding out if (a) the informant became bored with constant repetition and therefore blocked receptive capability, or (b) if constant repetition led to increased concern and interest. Especially in this area of investigation we expected emotional strategies. Attitudes, political opinions, prejudices and motivation all determine the updating process. News stories are evaluated, qualified and put into categories immediately; and to be integrated at all they must have something to do with one's own experience.

A young female doctor gave us a very straightforward, honest set of replies, similar to her statements in other parts of the interview:

> A: Eh – how do you feel about the Lebanon? News about the Lebanon?

B: That is all somehow so sad and so confusing. So.

A: Eh – isn't there something new almost every day?

B: Yes – there is always news on the conflict Iran–Iraq – Lebanon conflict. Where you really know somehow – that is such a terrible – awful war – where – I myself – due to my lack of extensive political knowledge – cannot even explain – why they fight each other. And – the day – today developments I find less interesting – but what really troubles me is to hear – that the war is still continuing. Or so.

A: Mhm – eh – how is it, for instance, – ah – when you hear such reports on the Lebanon? Can you integrate them into – a – into a schema – or a knowledge of – what you already know?

B: Yes – just about. But if they blow up the American Embassy once more or so – I mean – that is somehow just a continuation of atrocities – you hear about.

A: How has that developed in Lebanon? Who fights whom – and why – how does that work?

B: The Christians against the others or something like that. But why it is – sometime ago I studied it in a workshop – but – (..........)

A: Well – how does it affect you – when you hear about it? One side throws a bomb – and then the other. Do you even know – who both sides are?

B: What I do not know is – who the good ones are, and who the bad ones are. For which side should we keep our fingers crossed? What should we be pleased about and what not – I mean. Somehow – if I listen at all – then – my thoughts are associating – that I think – so crazy – that they still continue the war – they ought to make peace at last – their country is beautiful – and they could live well there. But at the same time somehow. What – what is it to me – when they wipe each other out in Lebanon? I can do nothing against it and all it does is remind me – that there is still a war going on there. But there is nothing we can do from here. I don't even know which side to support.

A: Ah – you do listen to such reports? – On Lebanon? Or do you avoid the reports or are you –

B: It is just – that I know so little about it. Perhaps it would be different – if I had ever been there – but – no, not avoid, not really. But I don't actually concentrate on such reports – well – I rather close my eyes to them. I mean – with Sri Lanka, that's different . . .

(Text 8; Interview 13:10–12) (middle class, doctor, female)

This excerpt suggests something of the function and effect of such news reports on the development of consciousness, even if the audience does not always listen carefully ('But I don't actually concentrate on such reports'), or cannot coordinate all the facts ('who the good ones are, and who the bad ones are'). Her statement that 'That is all somehow so sad and so confusing', reveals her obvious bewilderment. Contradictory strategies are applied. She tries to evaluate, but confesses to not knowing enough about it. And she feels helpless as well. Everything is senseless, nothing can be done – so why form an opinion at all? The line of argumentation here is typical and indicates the strong emotional involvement in, but also the barriers to, listening and understanding what is 'really going on'.

In the texts from working-class informants this tendency towards emotional reaction is even more pronounced. The interviewee is male, a decorator, and the subject is the situation in Lebanon:

A: Eh – recently – there are also – frequently reports of various sorts on Lebanon. Another truce concluded – another truce broken. Then again someone is blown sky-high. Or something like that. How do you feel – when you hear such reports – from Lebanon?

B: Well – if you want to know my opinion – I can only say one thing – on Lebanon. – I was together with a Lebanese. In – a different prison. And – he told me a bit about it. – I mean, about all those wars over there. About all the political parties – which exist there. And they fight each other. And – who – there are several, you know. I tell myself – why is a world power like America – or France or England not prepared to – they should just go down there. Rrumps! Hit them hard. Why, why were we arrested? Because they want to get rid of us – see. Just hit them hard, they – could – just once – to bring an end to it all. Then there'll be nothing more to report for a time – see. And it'll all be quiet there – see. That is how I see it. That is my opinion – see. Because – if they are a Super Power – what do I know – then let them go down there just once – force peace on them – to keep them from fighting each other. And only make it worse. And it spreads and spreads. I really just don't understand it. That is warmongering. Just warmongering pure and simple.

A: Mhm – mhm.

B: Because the French have pulled out – for instance. They were there – long enough. They pulled out – just – because they go on fighting there – see.

A: Yes, yes.

B: And that – even more get killed there.

A: Yes – sure – and – eh – are you really sure – who fights against whom and why?

B: Well – I don't want to say much – because I – because I am not very well-informed about this subject. But – I do know – that – for instance – who knows – that very many are involved – I am not so well informed. But – ah – with the –

A: We hear such different things all the time.

B: That is why – when I am not very well informed on a subject – then – I don't want to talk so much – so as not to appear idiotic or something. – – All I can say – the only thing – which I – a basic principle – know – the way I judge it – it is perverse – what they are doing there. It is simply perverse – I mean – it ought to be ended – period. And finished – see. But if a terrorist – he has learned a trade – they break him, too – see. They cannot continue either – continue their bomb attacks and so on. Therefore the same should be done there. There are umpteen million people there – or what – I don't know – how many there are – umpteen million. But – there are plenty of people – who want to be left in peace, at the end of the day. Who want to live – who want to work. Who have children – see. And then they spread their propaganda everywhere – hunger – see. Hunger – death – and so on. Thirst – and why – because – there is only war – see.

A: Mhm – mhm – well – I mean – eh – when you hear such reports – on Lebanon – eh – eh – how do you handle them? Can you somehow integrate them into your world view? Or – or – do you just say – that – I just don't listen any longer?

B: Correct.

A: Or –

B: I have reached the point – where I think – that is all the same to me. Let them bump each other off. Let them get rid of each other. If they think that it is right – and if it is organized – that, too. Well – what kind of a picture am I to – to make of it – for myself? I can only say – you please yourselves – I do not listen any longer. I am not even interested any longer. That is my opinion. All right – somebody else has a different opinion. He might think – oh well – it could be done in such and such a way. But all that smuggling of arms – and their little deals this way and that – just so that they can fight. And the other side can fight back. No sense in it. Well – no sense in it at all at the end of the day.

(Text 32; Interview 29:10–12) (working class, decorator, male)

The interviewee does not need to be asked specific questions for him to express very strong opinions and develop strategies for the termination of the conflict that could hardly be more direct in their practicality ('Rrumps! Hit them hard'). He connects these strategies with his present situation ('Because they want to get rid of us') which he obviously considers reasonable. On the other hand, the description of the situation acquires a poetical – and also accusatory – dimension ('Hunger – death – and so on. Thirst – and why – because – there is only war – see'). This becomes less credible, though, when he makes his counterproposals ('Hit them'). Prejudices and preconceived ideas are also dominant (he draws conclusions, uses clichés); in short, such arguments are typical of a prejudiced discourse (see Wodak *et al.* 1990).

The interviewee openly admits that the situation is unclear to him ('because I am not very well-informed about this subject'), and continuous war-reports from Lebanon have clearly taken the edge off his interest ('that is all the same to me', 'I am not even interested any longer'). What is especially relevant in this excerpt is the fact that the interviewee spontaneously, without waiting to be asked, offers his own preconceived ideas. When addressing specific conflict-laden themes it is more important for him to voice his views than to put forward any rational argument. Thus, the information is immediately interpreted in terms of his own prejudices, and updating, in the sense of *actualité*, does not occur. This attitude is typical of many interviewees: they believe themselves to be more or less well-informed, but when asked precise questions, have to admit to knowing very little, really. Is the feeling of participating in world affairs a pure illusion on the part of the listener or viewer? Such a feeling certainly seems to inform the audience's attitudes and opinions, whereas cognitive processing depends strongly on background knowledge and a motivation to acquire knowledge. Many interviewees are seeking confirmation; they wait for those pieces of information that conform to their own prejudices.

For the majority of those few 'privileged' listeners – privileged because of their high degree of social integration and education – the reformulation of news texts (simplified syntax, increased semantic coherence) led to some improvement in comprehension. However, we are then confronted with the problem that those subjects who understood a great deal to start with seem to profit far more from the reformulations than those who had not understood very much initially. Thus the gap widens, even though a slight increase in comprehension can be observed all along the line.

Here the limits of the applications of sociolinguistic research become apparent: the use of purely linguistic means can simplify the presentation of information and cognitive processing, but it is powerless to eliminate deficiencies and differences in education and knowledge (social integration in different environments resulting in different 'worlds' and thus leading to different interests, priorities, etc.). If, for example, a person is ignorant of the fact that Lebanon and Iran are two different countries (which does not seem to be a rare 'gap'), no news report, however intelligibly presented, is able to transmit new knowledge, but will at best reinforce vague prejudices, or simply remain unassimilable, hence unassimilated or ignored. Consequently, the social problem of the unintelligibility of the news must be contextualized alongside other key tasks of education. Students in contemporary Austria hardly learn to listen to the news, much less interpret it. The discourse genre 'news', including its characteristic specialized language, should be dealt with in schools, and students should be trained to make a critical evaluation of the political information presented.

In addition, factual relevance and subjective interest are factors of great significance: the relationship between subjective interest and the quality of the interview material actually produced is clearly visible. The more interesting the topic to the interviewee, the better the reproduction performance. However, few topics were of sufficient interest. This is surely due not only to the nature of the information and personalities involved, even though it is possible to show that personal involvement or the relevance of news items to one's daily life do help make it more comprehensible. Binding elements (cohesion, coherence) as well as links to a relevant report from the previous day or week are often missing in a given text. The audience hears fragments – 'intertextuality' was non-existent or only barely explicit, often making it impossible for an embedding of information in background knowledge to take place. Programme-makers should also consider developing the interest of the audience through additional information programmes (perhaps following the brief reports, for example), in which foreign vocabulary, special terminology and the use of abbreviations, which are often criticized by the audience, could be explained in context. Contradictions between individual news items could also be explained, thereby enabling the listener or viewer better to assemble the fragments into a coherent whole.

Only if the audience is able to process the news in context and evaluate its implications and consequences will it become of interest. Only then will it be possible for the audience to evaluate in a critical way the material presented to it (i.e. with respect to its truth and function), and thus become self-confident active users and not merely passive consumers of the modern media.

Notes

1. In this book, I will not include a very similiar study on legal texts and discourse because our analysis of news discourse illustrates and exemplifies the methodology and also the kind of results achieved (Pfeiffer/Strouhal/Wodak 1987). The same socio-cognitive model was applied, comprehension and comprehensibility of legal texts tested. The legal texts were again reformulated, and the new texts were compared with the original in a sequence of tests. The results obtained in the study of legal discourse confirms our results in the study presented here: the social gap widens and inequality is further stabilized.

2. The news broadcasts and also newspapers take over the story genre provided by the news agency. Benke (1994) showed how information is transported from the agency clipping into the official news text, which information is quoted and which neglected.

3. 'Sauha' is an abbreviation for 'sauhaufen', meaning 'garbage' or 'dumpster' colloquially.

4. The sample consisted of 277 informants who were tested in 13 grades, in four different types of school (high schools, high schools with a focus on mathematics, high schools with a focus on business, and schools for apprentices). There were 128 women and 149 men. The class-structure coincides with the types of schools chosen: high schools have middle-class and lower-middle-class students, the schools for apprentices are mostly attended by working-class students. All the informants were between the ages of 16 to 18. (For details see Lutz/Wodak 1987: 94 ff.)

5. Fifty interviews were done: the interviewees were aged between 18 and 73; half were male, half female. 25 informants were middle class, 20 were lower-middle class, and 5 were from the working class (defined by income, education and profession).

5 'Self-reflection and emancipation?' Sociolinguistic aspects of the therapeutic process and its effect

5.1 Linguistics and psychotherapy

The interest of linguistics in therapeutic communication has greatly increased in recent years,[1] starting in 1977, with the publication of Labov and Fanshel's study *Therapeutic Discourse*. The reasons for this lie on the one hand in the development of pragmatics and speech act theory, and on the other in the goal of dealing with authentic empirical material from therapy case studies. Because of its precisely defined setting and its rules, and above all because of the significant differences compared with everyday conversations, the material from therapeutic situations makes it possible to explain important fundamental conditions of human communication. From a methodological point of view, it makes sense to use material from 'extreme' and restricted situations, as it is easier to understand and analyse everyday communication in comparison with such inter-actions (Drew/Heritage 1992). Moreover, the language-game 'therapy' is a speech situation in which action is almost exclusively verbal, with the aim of intended self-reflection and change. It thus involves communication directly connected to human and social practice. It is exactly here that we pose the question raised in 1.5: Can distorted communication be changed? And what are the consequences: New disorders? More subtle disorders? Or more understanding?

5.2 Therapeutic communication in groups

5.2.1 *The investigation*

In my own longitudinal investigation of therapeutic communication in groups at the Crisis Intervention Centre in Vienna, I recorded therapy sessions on tape over a period of three years and examined them from a variety of perspectives.

5.2.1.1 *The course of the project*

Data for the study were collected over the period of 1976–78. The study divides into eight characteristic phases:

1   **Familarization with the institution:** I started by spending three months as a trainee at the Vienna Crisis Intervention Centre, where I was given a wide range of tasks. I filled out filing cards, accompanied the therapist in open groups, answered the telephone, and sometimes spoke with waiting patients. I soon got to know the habits, values and everyday life of the institution by asking questions, observing, and reading doctors' reports.

2   **Preliminary study:** After I had observed the open group several times and become used to the communication structures, I recorded four sessions on tape.

3   **Pilot study:** These four tapes were subjected to preliminary analysis, and the general hypotheses were elaborated and refined. Individual phases of the sessions required further analysis and were dealt with separately (Wodak-Leodolter 1977).

4   **Main investigation:** After I had carried out the pilot study, elaborated my hypotheses, and studied further literature, I embarked on the main phase of the investigation. In the course of two months, starting exactly a year after the first recording, I recorded on tape 16 sessions of the same group. My aim was to obtain a broader database and make it possible to investigate the effect of the therapy.

5   **Notes:** At the same time, I made notes of non-verbal reactions. I was also able to look at the doctors' notes at regular intervals and was always given the opportunity to confer with the team.

6   **Interviews with patients:** In focused interviews, ten patients

were asked about their subjective evaluation of the therapy. To this end, I visited individual patients in their homes, with their consent. I thus had an opportunity to get to know their language behaviour outside the therapeutic situation and to find out more about their lives and social environment.

7   **Interviews with therapists:** I also interviewed a psychiatrist, two psychologists and a female social worker on their attitudes toward the therapeutic method and its chances of success, and on their opinions on the institution as a whole.

8   **Analysis and interpretation:** Finally, I carried out a qualitative and quantitative analysis using all the sources of data at my disposal (recorded sessions, notes and interviews). Even during this phase, I never lost contact with the institution: I repeatedly conferred, received new information, and reported on provisional results.

5.2.2 The ethical dilemma in the research of therapeutic communication

The ethnographic method and the insider-perspective are most important in order to obtain genuine and authentic data. Nevertheless, as we know from many sociolinguistic studies, the observer paradox is inevitable and certainly distorts the authenticity of the situation considerably. Thus, researchers have to find strategies to cope with this paradox: for example, ensuring that the researcher is already known to the informants over some time, and that he or she is introduced by somebody connected to the situation. The informants need to be assured that the tape recorder could be switched off, as soon as they request that. And thirdly, informants should also have access to the tapes if they want to listen to them as well. Research has shown that after a period of five to ten minutes, the existence of the tape recorder is often forgotten, and the informants give free rein to their emotions (Labov 1966, Wodak-Leodolter/ Dressler 1978, Dressler/Wodak 1981).[2]

I spoke to the patients about the aims of the therapy and the investigation, and assured them of anonymity. I was soon accepted and integrated, particularly after the interviews that I conducted in the homes of individual patients. There I had an opportunity to study their way of life more closely. Awareness of people's personal circumstances facilitates considerable insight into their personalities, making it easier to understand their individual suffering and personal history. Patients displayed remarkably few inhibitions during the interviews. On the contrary, they had a great urge to describe their problems to me, even though many of those were of an intimate nature. I was somehow forced into a therapeutic role, since I had previously appeared together with the therapist.

I was particularly pleased when the patients invited me to eat with them after the therapy sessions (thus integrating me into the group). The patients opened up in the congenial atmosphere of these informal gatherings; they cracked jokes, talked about their daily lives, and asked me about my work and my views on everyday problems. They also asked about the research, since, with the permission of the Crisis Intervention Centre, I regularly gave them articles and brief interim reports to read. In this way I managed to reduce the distance between investigator and subject. The patients expressed markedly contradictory feelings towards the research. Some displayed tremendous faith in academic knowledge ('Go ahead and make the recordings – they will help our children'), and others were proud to participate in a scientific study. In fact, those patients were almost offended at being identified only by numbers or social class instead of by name. Others, by contrast, were distrustful and questioning. They insisted on having the tapes played back to them to check what they had said and see whether they had been correctly understood. Two women in particular felt self-conscious at times; on occasion they would explicitly refer to the tape recorder (they were 'unable' to say things because someone was listening); at other times they would become excited and aggressive, swearing and afterward apologizing to the tape recorder. Before every session I asked the patients for permission to turn on the tape recorder. Often it took a full five minutes of discussion (though the therapist never intervened) before they were able to reach agreement. I was frequently asked to talk about my research interest, a request that I was naturally happy to meet.

Only once was I refused permission to make a recording, on the day before Christmas, when patients referred to the forthcoming festivities. Naturally, I obliged and did not switch the recorder on. I remained for the session to demonstrate my interest not only in the recordings but also – and above all – in the patients themselves. Incidentally, while this session was not structurally different from others, the patients' request did bring to light the latent stress produced by the recordings.

It was relatively difficult to establish contact with the patients during the preliminary study. During the main study I tried to enter the therapy room before the others, without the therapist (on the pretext of setting up the tape recorder). This enabled me to gain familiarity with pre-therapy talk, and as a result I was drawn into the discussion. These minor events made it easier for me to overcome the ethical problems. One big problem of course is the fact that an essential part of the therapy is the maintenance of anonymity and – particularly in individual therapy – the consideration that no uninvolved person should be admitted. In fact, I consider it inadmissible to break this constitutive rule of individual therapy. A different ethical problem is encountered in group therapy, where the presence of observers can be of theoretical and practical value. It is never possible to avoid this ethical dilemma. One can, however, reduce one's misgivings, mainly by attempting to establish personal contact with the patients. It helps to tell them about the aims of the investigation and allows them to take part in the research process.

5.2.3 Descriptions of the data

5.2.3.1 The institution: Vienna Crisis Intervention Centre

The problem of suicide and the various theories on the subject cannot be adequately described here; nor is any priority attached to the institutional aspect of the treatment of mentally ill patients and potential suicide candidates. We are interested here solely in one aspect of therapeutic treatment, the open group. Patients may join the 'open group' even when therapy has already started, whereas 'closed groups' do not admit new members. Till (1977) has already referred to institutional questions in his study of the efficiency of the entire institution; Gernot Sonneck, on the other hand, writes about the intentions and goals of crisis intervention:

> Crisis intervention, or the psychosocial treatment of symptoms, illnesses and abnormal attitudes closely connected with crises, can be carried out either outside the professional system by relatives, friends or acquaintances, priests, teachers, social welfare workers and family doctors, or within the professional system. The latter covers a wide

range of institutions, from consulting and welfare offices to the declared crisis intervention centre. (Sonneck 1976: 421)

Thus, the aim of such an institution is:

To enable people involved in crisis to mobilize their strength so that they can solve their problems given suitable assistance ... It must be possible to achieve the aim of intervention within a short space of time, a change of personality not being the primary objective. Neither should the objective be a return to the status quo ante, but the achievement of a more stable condition by helping the individuals to help themselves. (Sonneck 1976: 421)

These statements are particularly important, as they clearly define the goal of the therapeutic group. This does not involve a fundamental psychoanalytical therapy, but a symptom-oriented method suitable for the treatment of serious crises. Over and above this, the group also discusses conflicts and transference problems but these are of secondary importance.

Farberow describes in detail various attempts at instituting group therapy in crisis intervention:

In the interaction during the hour, the therapists are directing, questioning, guiding. If time permits, everyone is encouraged to talk and to interact with each other, i.e., both seek help and give it. The role reversals are impressive. Some of the most intractable problems simply disappear as the same person directs his or her attention to someone else and becomes his or her counsellor. The focus is on the (here and now), or what is occurring in the patient's life which is stimulating the suicidal impulses. (Farberow 1973: 13)

Farberow goes on to say that, 'Despite the conceptualization of the "drop-in" session as non-group, it has been interesting to note the strong tendencies toward group formation', and reminds us that 'the goal with the patients in the "drop-in" sessions is to identify with the centre'. This means less responsibility for patients than in a truly closed group, although, as described above, the typical patterns and mechanisms of a therapeutic group are immediately established. Identification with the institution rather than with a group or a therapist is a temporary solution. The success rate of the open group is very high (Farberow 1973, Strauss/Sonneck 1978).

In the case of the Vienna Crisis Intervention Centre, the group meets four times a week in the evening, Fridays excepted (when there are afternoon sessions). Specific therapists take the group on certain days. Patients may choose the therapist whose therapeutic style they like best or, in acute crisis, they can obtain daily support. I limited my recordings to two therapists (one female, one male) so as to keep the variable of therapist constant. Despite the fluctuation of patients, there was a core group of about 12 patients during the three years of the investigation. Eleven patients were there only occasionally, but they did maintain a presence throughout the duration of the study.

There are several reasons for my decision to observe and record the open group rather than the 'closed group'. First, the ethical problem with the latter would have been much greater. Second – and this is very important – we are interested primarily in analysis at the colloquial level, where prime importance is attached not to transference phenomena but to real problems as such. Latent levels always play a role as well and will also be included but are initially of secondary importance in the therapy (see below 5.2.4). As a result, the open group can provide the necessary information about therapeutic discourse as there is no major difference between it and a 'purely' psychotherapeutic group with regard to the institutional background and the interaction patterns within the group, particularly in view of the characteristic metacommunication.[3]

The team consists of a manager, four doctors, three psychologists, five social workers, a music therapist and – for all eventualities – a lawyer. The psychologists, one doctor and the social workers are employed there full-time. The centre works on a team principle, which means that all team members carry out the same work and accept the same responsibility, but to varying extents depending on their training. This is so far the only centre of its kind in Vienna. About 1500 new patients are contacted every year (60% women, 40% men). The number of direct individual contacts is approximately 100 per month, of whom about one-third remain in the care of the centre. Altogether the social workers make about 1,800 home and hospital visits in the course of a year and register 6,000 calls; the psychologists, about 1,000 calls and about the same number of individual therapeutic sessions; the doctors, 600 first interviews and 2,500 individual therapy sessions.

A wide range of therapeutic forms is offered: open and closed groups, medical and psychotherapy, short-term therapy, and meditation. All treatment is available on the national health service, and, as a result, the sample embraces patients from every social class. Most patients are aged between 30 and 60, and about two-thirds of the patients are women. Patients come on their own initiative (the centre is open daily from ten in the morning until ten at night; during the night there is an answering service) or, after an attempted suicide, they are referred to the centre by the psychiatric clinic, which does not offer crisis intervention. The average number of visits per patient is more than four; in the open group, about nine. Every week the professional team itself meets for a joint session, which I was always able to take part in, when problems of demanding patients were discussed. The supervisory staff of the centre themselves form a therapeutic group, meeting every two weeks to discuss the problems that inevitably occur in such strenuous work. The institution is undergoing expansion as part of the restructuring and reorganization of psychiatric services in Vienna.

5.2.3.2 *The random sample*

The random sample compared 23 patients whom I observed and recorded in 20 sessions over the course of three years. It was broken down by social class: five women and three men were middle class; three women and four men were lower-middle class; and four women and four men were working class. The criterion for determination of class was an index based on profession, education and income. Women who did not work were classified by their training and background. Each patient was given a number that was retained for all analysis and description. I differentiated among three age groups (under 25, 26 to 40, over 40) and three types of education (primary school, secondary school, higher education). Classification by social class had to be carried out on the basis of status before the illness, as many patients were unemployed during their crisis, so realistic classification on the basis of present status was impossible.

Although I do not wish to make any statistical assertions, one point is clear: most of the contributions (turns) (see 5.3.4 below) came from middle-class women of the middle age group.

Only '**problem presentation in group therapy**' was included in both quantitative and qualitative analysis. These are turns dealing with a topic that arouses deep emotions of the patient concerned and is complete in itself. The length of the contributions was also taken into account in the quantitative evaluation. A more detailed description of the genre selected is given in the appropriate passage dealing with the qualitative analysis of the text corpus in the light of our hypotheses (see below 5.3.1). The problems dealt with in a total of 1,134 turns relate to nine topics: (1) contact, (2) work, (3) medication, (4) group metalevel, i.e. discussion of relationships within the group, (5) group activities, (6) illness, (7) children, (8) parents, and (9) relationships.

A number of interesting questions emerge from this distribution pattern, leading to a differentation of the general hypotheses with regard to class- and gender-specific differences:

1 Women talk more than men.
2 The problems mainly dealt with by women are different from those of men. Regardless of social class, problems relating to children, parents and relationships are more 'women's' problems, while men tend to talk about problems in the group and at work.
3 The various social classes deal with different problems and there are gender-specific differences within each class as well.

These hypotheses are tested in the overall quantitative analysis (see Wodak 1986a). These quantitative differences raise interesting problems, such as the explicit description of the interplay of class and gender based on the indicator of topic selection.

5.2.3.3 Examples of text topics [4]

The symbols T (therapist), W (woman), and M (man) are used throughout to indicate participants.

Text 1. Topic 1: contact. Session 4, patient 20 (male)

Contact with other people somehow makes me nervous. I also find that when I go to the group, I am sort of jittery all day about going. On the other hand, I want and look for contact with people.

Text 2. Topic 2: work. Session 4, patient 15 (male)

With whom and how I work. So that is really what the present problem is about, with whom I manage, you see. That is important, but things are already better than before. The only thing that upsets me is number one, with the harassment, which I have already mentioned; number two is, let's say, I react in such a negative way to people who violently – no, not violently – who start shouting that – well I can put up with everything, both in my job and in my private life, just not people shouting at me. If someone shouts at me, I can lose my composure. I can completely lose my composure. My entire self-confidence disappears, do you understand? I can put up with it up to a certain limit, but when somebody shouts at me, for me he becomes a sort of, say, not God, but a big shot compared with me, you see, just because he has shouted at me. He always seems so immensely large compared with me, a tiny little nothing.

Text 3. Topic 3: medication. Session 6, patient 1 (female)

And you were in the Monday group and told us about your suicide attempt, and when I got home I just couldn't handle it. That's how it actually happened. It was a Sunday, or a Tuesday – at any rate, a day on which I went to Bisamberg [a mountain near Vienna] with the last strength I could muster; I could only walk to Bisamberg, and so I took a suppository to help me make it and noticed how I was using my reserves and it became clear to me that this suicide is a question of time, you see? It's just a question of time – 'how long you can still hold out, how long you can still go on' – then I collapsed yet again. Here, you saw me too, – then I had taken such a strong dose – and I thought to myself, 'now you must stop at once,' and so I rang the doctor and told him. Now it's Tuesday, Wednesday, Thursday, Friday, Saturday, Sunday, Monday, the seventh day since the great crisis, but still, it's pretty bad.

Text 4. Topic 4: group metalevel. Session 4, patient 16 (male)

May I say something? Well, I have noticed that the start of the group ... that the man began with this problem; in her reply the woman immediately mentioned the problem and gave of her best. You in turn gave an answer with your problem, and – everyone just talks about their problem. Only I think that – I think we should – I imagine that we should talk about it a bit, go into it more, if we – we can't solve it anyway.

Text 5. Topic 5: group activities. Session 4, patient 11 (female)

Me? Yes, I have also got something to say, but it is something quite different now /cough/, and that is that some time ago I had an idea that I would like to put into practice; I have often been in the psychiatric hospital at Steinhof to visit somebody, and I have always been moved by the people, by the situation there. I don't know whether you know, but there was an article in *Profil* [a weekly magazine], and my idea is that we could introduce some culture into the hospital, and I want to encourage the people from the old Arena [an arts group of the late seventies] to give a performance there, for younger people and for the sick ...

Text 6. Topic 6: illness. Session 1, patient 16 (male)

M: I dream a lot anyway, about things, about psychiatrists and mental hospitals, and I think that – that has not yet – Gugging [a psychiatric hospital] – I've not yet really got over it, in my psyche, where I was ill. I don't know – straitjackets, then this guy collapsed, and bleeding and –
W: Perhaps it's because you think about it all the time, that you're maybe depressive, that it's always there, that –
M: That was not easy, being in the loony bin twice, but – and I, I am aware that I'll certainly never go back there, but still, I didn't know whether or not I would get out, things are so terrible there, I dream about that, too, and I think that the background to my dreams, that I think – all that has its origin. I often dream about drugs, you know, which was also a terrible experience. I often dream about the loony bin; that was also a terrible experience, you know.

Text 7. Topic 7: children. Session 19, patient 5 (female)

The youngest, he was 13, and there was a particularly good relationship, which was terribly complicated for me, because I had to run all over the place with him, and at that time he went to the planetarium almost two or three times a week and also assumed that everybody knew anyway what's up above, you know, and he said, 'People explain that all so primitively; I know all that anyway,' and then he asked me questions, and I sat up at night and learned it so that I would not disappoint him and have to tell him, 'Dear, that's ...'

Text 8. Topic 8: parents. Session 19, patient 5 (female)

Well, she [mother] talks with him [father] anyway. I can't even stand him any more. I mean, we met last Sunday, I couldn't even [stand] his presence – four metres away I could stand and breathe – well, I mean – and I – you can't even describe it, I, I mean, everybody in the group has their own cross to bear, perhaps a worse one, but at the moment that is always the reproach, I can – it's just impossible to talk to my father at all, because if I say, 'Look – at the moment he is being treated by Dr X [doctor's name] I already told you – by Dr X [doctor's name], then I said, 'Why didn't you go there this week?' Well, I shouldn't have said that, for example, but, well, I'm just about alright, and I take the pills, and I can't talk at the moment, and and Dr X [doctor's name] doesn't say either – I mean, I really would like to help, too – You get such a lot of words when you have six patients and talk an hour with each –I mean, he wouldn't do that. You know yourself that psychiatrists just [speak] a few words, and so – they speak, but don't – he can't say, put that in a glass of water . . .

Text 9. Topic 9: relationships. Session 3, patient 8 (female)

Yes, alright: I have found a friend, my fiancé, and we broke up because he went back to his wife and child, but he wanted to phone me once a week or more, to ask how I was. Somehow I'm still very fond of the man. He calls up and asks how I am. He upsets my life. Now I've forbidden him to do that, and I hope that I'll be able to get over it now with Mr X [person's name], that he'll help me, that he'll take care of me, and that he'll also get out with me, so that I'm back in society and so that I can't think about it so much. I wanted to know whether that's a good thing, or whether I'd better leave things as they are.

I shall continue by outlining the discourse model, which allows us to record the diversity of therapeutic communication in groups, and then examine the therapeutic effect by means of an illustrative text analysis of two passages spoken by the same female patient at the beginning and at the end of the therapy. I shall analyse these in the light of a single indicator: 'narrative structure'. Further information, a description of other methods and categories used, and the results of an analysis of class- and gender-specific speech behaviour can be found in Wodak (1981a, 1981b, 1986a) and in Wodak/Schulz (1986).

5.2.4 The 'three-level model' of therapeutic communication in groups

5.2.4.1 A new conception of 'meaning'

Therapeutic discourse in groups is a complex phenomenon. Its diversity is the result of three factors: the actual communication and group dynamics that take place (the 'here and now'), the 'family transference', and the expectations and life history of the individual. It follows that verbal interaction and communication reflect these three factors.

As a result, verbal expressions and texts in a therapeutic situation are made up of three significant components: colloquial meaning, which is based on membership of a speech community; group meaning, which relates the value of what is said to the latent transference level in the group; and, finally, personal semantics, the expression of the individual's life history, psychogenesis and pathogenesis, and the position of the patient in the social structure of society. A threefold interpretation frame by itself, therefore, offers a satisfactory means of recording and interpreting the complete significance of therapeutic discourse.

Figure 5.1 shows the 'three-level model', the linguistic dimensions necessary to analyse and understand therapeutic discourse.

5.2.4.2 The colloquial meaning

This level involves expressions in a group-therapy situation that can be explicitly comprehended in their everyday colloquial sense. Patients describe their problems, discuss the activities of the group, discuss relationships, and settle conflicts (Wodak 1981a: 113ff.). Although everything that occurs in a therapeutic situation has particular significance for the group process and the individual (latent meaning), attention is focused initially on the text as such, without further analysis or interpretation. As the technique of the 'open group' for suicide candidates aims to treat real problems, the use of colloquial meaning for analysis is necessary and legitimate.

5.2.4.3 Group specific meaning

In order to avoid possible misunderstanding, it should be emphasized from the start that we are dealing here not with a completely

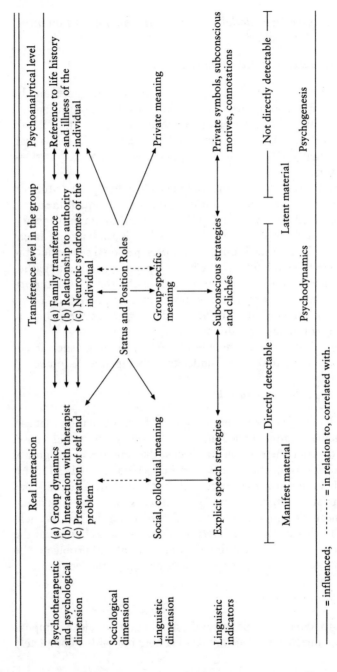

Figure 5.1: Interaction levels in group therapy*

different language or with another dialogue that has taken place simultaneously, but with a second dimension of meaning that allows us to interpret the meaning of each expression with reference to the dynamics of the group. A second set of categories obtained from the theories of group processes is applied to the text (Bion 1961, Kutter 1971, Grumiller 1975, Finger 1976, Slater 1978). Owing to the peculiarities of the therapeutic setting, many of the transference factors of individual patients are manifest in the group situation, in their relationship to one another and to the therapist. Typical group structures and processes, hierarchies and conflicts develop, though, initially at least, this normally remains unnoticed. Each utterance by an individual participant must therefore be analysed with respect not only to its colloquial meaning, but also to its value and function in a group context. What did the speaker intend to achieve by his or her utterance? Why did he or she address a particular member of the group? Why does a conflict occur between two people? Finger (1976: 91) attempts to integrate the various group concepts; all the phenomena mentioned here manifest themselves in typical verbal expressions (including symbols or clichés).

To the extent that the process of integration within the group is also a process of eliminating linguistic subversion, it is more than a formal repetition of the infantile process of socialization. With the reconstruction of language a process begins that allows the private language of each individual to become gradually incorporated into the linguistic community. This is equivalent to a contextually new process of socialization that makes it possible to transform old interactive forms into new ones and allows old methods of solving conflicts to be replaced by new and better ones (Finger 1976: 91).

5.2.4.4 *Private meaning*

Communication in a group conceals yet another aspect besides that of manifestly comprehensible verbal language and group meaning. The verbal utterances of each individual carry for him or her particular associations, his or her own connotations that can be understood only in the context of his or her life history and expectations.

The small child learns linguistic behaviour through interaction with a primary parental figure. The experience gained in these first interactions has a cognitive and emotional effect on the small child.

Although in the course of time the child learns to abstract these interactions, the emotional component of his first experiences remains, and is passed on. Colloquial speech-games invariably have a private component.

Private meanings and private language are clearly apparent in psychotic patients, particularly schizophrenics (Leodolter 1975b). In my own investigation of schizophrenic speech behaviour, I found that the so-called 'disturbed' speech of these patients had quite different structures, similiar to the mechanisms of dream texts, or in other words unconscious material. This private language can be translated back into colloquial language using psychotherapeutic methods (Green 1974). As a result, neurotic people – and even normal people – introduce their private symbols and connotations into everyday speech acts, though they are not as apparent as in the case described above.

In a group it is not only group dynamics that play a decisive role, but also the psychogenesis and pathogenesis of the individual, the expectations of the individual, his or her experiences and knowledge. When understood in a broader sense, private linguistic elements are only apparent against the background of each life history and the history of individual object relationships, which cannot be perceived from observation of the group situation alone. The most one can do, therefore, is to establish hypotheses that can be tested with the help of individual therapy. Detailed discussion of the linguistic analysis of connotations would exceed the remit of this chapter.

5.3 Qualitative text analysis: the therapeutic effect

5.3.1 *Problem presentation in group therapy*

Like therapeutic discourse, the genre in which we are chiefly interested – **'problem presentation in group therapy'** – also involves several levels of meaning. Not only is the manifest content significant, but also the context (at what time during the session a problem is discussed) and, finally, the motives that induce an individual patient to describe a problem in a particular manner (see Figure 5.2).

Problem presentation in group therapy involves lengthy sections of monologue during which a patient expresses a personal problem.

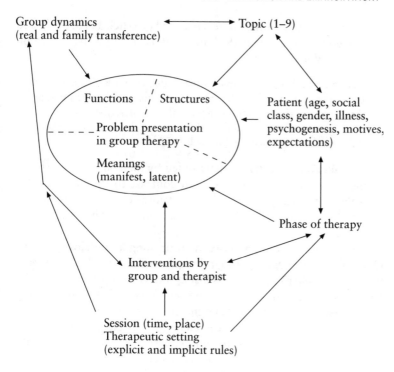

Group dynamics
(real and family transference)

Topic (1–9)

Functions / Structures

Problem presentation
in group therapy

Meanings
(manifest, latent)

Patient (age, social
class, gender, illness,
psychogenesis, motives,
expectations)

Phase of therapy

Interventions by
group and therapist

Session (time, place)
Therapeutic setting
(explicit and implicit rules)

Figure 5.2: The Position of Problem Presentation in Group Therapy in Therapeutic Discourse

The passages of text subjected to analysis also extend to the immediate reaction of the group or therapist, and to the patient's answer (we are thus dealing with an interaction unit) (see example above). The questions and hypotheses elaborated were tested in the light of a quantitative analysis of 1,134 problems presented in group therapy.

5.3.2 The 'narrative structure'

This category is used to describe the text structure (of a discourse strategy). Typical forms of problem presentation in group therapy can be divided into three subcategories: 'scene', 'narration' and 'circumstance'. The indicators selected are 'speaker's perspective' (Werlich 1975: 46ff.), the presence (or absence) of metacommunicative speaker strategies, the narrative tense used (Werlich 1975: 51ff), and the coherence of the text (Kallmeyer *et al.* 1974: 57ff) of certain utterances which

> contain a number of constituents that indicate and limit the root of the viewpoint from which the speakers in a communicative situation and to which all subjects, changes and facts described in the text refer. Text constituents that fulfil this function clarify various aspects of the speaker's perspective. (Werlich 1975: 46)

The speaker's perspective is determined by 'person' (i.e. the choice of the impersonal 'one' or 'you', in contrast to the personal 'I'), 'presentation' as a speaker's selective attitude to situational factors, 'focus', 'voice', 'genus' and 'mood' (Leodolter 1975b: 88ff; Wodak 1986a: 135ff).

A distinction is drawn between an opening and a closing focus. **Opening focus** refers to temporal sequences that gradually become more comprehensive, while **closing focus** comprises local and temporal sequential forms that become increasingly less comprehensive (Werlich 1975: 50). 'The choice of a **voice** [my emphasis] . . . indicates how the speaker sees changes and circumstances with reference to segments in the temporal continuum, or how she would like them to be seen. The speaker's perspective of the aspect is thus always closely linked to the choice of tenses' (p. 52).

Although in German, voice is expressed lexically rather than directly in the form of a verb, the marked and continuous aspect can nevertheless be differentiated. **Genus** refers to the choice of active or passive voice and indicates whether the speaker wishes to view changes and circumstances of phenomena as caused by him- or herself (i.e. with the speaker as an agent or as happening to him- or herself (p. 53). 'The choice of **mood** [my emphasis] . . . provides information about the entity attributed by the speaker to persons, objects and facts. There are three main moods from which the speaker can choose: the factual mood, the negative mood and the probable mood' (p. 54).

As will be shown, it is precisely in combination that these elements constitute an important criterion in differentiating the three text types.

The choice of the narrative tense is also an important indicator: 'The choice of the tense of a verb indicates how the speaker views objects and facts with relation to an axis of orientation formed by his/her momentary situation, i.e., by the speech act at any moment in time within the temporal continuum' (p. 51).

Finally, the coherence of the text affects the textual structure as a whole (Beaugrande/Dressler 1981: 88ff). Can speakers realize their intentions? Does the planned strategy achieve its goal, the desired reaction from the listener? Is the topic consistently pursued? Are references clear and comprehensible? According to Kallmeyer's definition, 'the coherence of dialogue results from connective elements, definition of the topic and the interactive context' (Kallmeyer *et al.* 1974: 58).

The indicators also naturally apply to longer monological sections, such as problem presentation in group therapy, in a wider interactive context. **Scene** is characterized by the absence of meta-communicative speaker strategies. It is a defined, personal speaker's perspective (use of 'I'). The presentation is highly selective (one event), the focus precise (unique experience). The aspect is marked (description of events). The voice is active, the mood factual. Scenes take place in the narrative present with much direct speech. Although there is coherence, the high degree of complexity coupled with the absence of metacommunicative signals make under-standing difficult for outsiders.

Narration refers to the classical narrative form of Labov and Waletzky (1967: 23). Orientation, complication, evaluation, resolu-tion and coda are present and ensure the coherence of the text. Orientation and evaluation provide its metacommunicative frame-work. The perspective of the definite, personal speaker comes to the fore. The focus closes (generalizations are normally possible only in connection with problem-solving). The aspect is marked, the mood factual. There is coherence, and – other patients permitting – a story will be related from beginning to end, though normally without direct connection to the problem being immediately established.

Circumstance refers to the description of a symptom, the circumstance of the speaker's suffering. In this case there is no metacommunicative frame. The speaker's perspective is impersonal (use of 'one' or 'you'); the focus opens. Problem presentation in group therapy is kept verbal and formal; the presentation is not selective. The aspect is unmarked (circumstance, continuity). The voice is passive, and the mood, finally, probable ('Perhaps it could ...'). The text is superficially coherent: a circumstance is described consistently, but much remains unclear to the listener because of the use of defence mechanisms; above all, there is no reference to the causes of the patient's case history – these are only implied. (In some instances it was necessary to use the wider context of the problem presentation in interpreting the text samples. Space considerations preclude explanation in detail here.)

Here are some examples of these three main types of narrative structure:

Working-class man, patient (M1). (Scene)

M1: Often I stand there and think I am being swallowed up by the earth, then I, then I can't see anything any more, I am quite gone [bin ganz weg] ... Yes, in private industry, I think you are really done for, because I am still free in a way. Not long ago I was up on the, up on the Ringturm, on the eighteenth floor, and I thought the whole, the whole – what do you call it, the thing you hold on to, you know –

M2: Railing?

M1: That's it, the railing would break; I got giddy again [des Wurlerte 'kriegt], and thought, should I jump, but then I went to the lift, went down, took a seat in a coffeehouse, and tried like mad to read. I ran round the block, but it didn't work, then I went again.

Middle-class man, patient. (Circumstance)

M: At the moment I really suffer from profuse sweating in the morning when I wake up and until I get up; it's so uncontrollable, and I'm completely washed out. My whole chest and everything is so tense. I'm working as a salesman again, and as I said, my boss is the nasty type. We've already had a difference of opinion, and when that happens, it happens then, especially in the morning; it's worst then.

T: What's your boss like, then?

M: Well, things may – things will probably settle down, but I still feel the first quarrel – it just came out of the blue. I know that when you're fifty you have to work harder than when you're young and let's say – to fill the job, anyway, everything is so tense that I can't get any rest. At the weekend I'm afraid, even on Friday, that the whole thing will start up again on Monday. But things are really going quite well, but I know, everything's alright, but the tension, this fear, the whole situation is terrible; it's disastrous for me. In the morning I'm completely whacked and I'm afraid of starting work again. So far I've only taken Deanxit, and not so many of them, at most one, and they don't help in my condition. I don't know – perhaps you can help me – if there's anything – a medication one can take.

Working-class woman, patient 9. (Scene)

W: So he says, 'That's got nothing to do with the others'; that's good for me when he says that. Now I can't even look at the paper. Then he says, 'You looking again? That's not for you, going out to work. And it's better for you if you stay at home, isn't it?' Then I say, 'I know you mean well, but you're trying to get your own way, because you want it.' Because, say, I went out to work in the afternoon, and my husband didn't like it, and because I couldn't have his tea waiting on the table for him. It's precooked anyway, and we've got a stove – all he has to do is heat it. And then I said, 'You don't want me to go because I can't serve your tea for you. You want it all your own way. You can't help me either, because I know that, too, when I get a job again, I'll be better off.'

Middle-class woman, patient (W1). (Narration)

W1: I'm afraid in the morning, too, afraid of failing at the office. And sometimes a certain fear of speaking in front of lots of people – that's why I don't find it very easy to talk (embarrassed laughter), but I know that such fear is often unfounded, but unfortunately I'm always afraid. I take Temesta, and that helps me a bit. Sometimes it's stronger and sometimes not so strong. I went through a time when I felt really groggy in the morning; I had to be sick, I had such an aversion, such a fear, a nausea until midday, and what happened until I was in a hectic state again –

W2: What are you actually afraid of?

W1: Well, now, let's say I had to type a very difficult text to begin with, and there are some people there, and I have to type, and now and again I make a spelling mistake in public – that would be very embarrassing for me, you know . . .

W2: Were you afraid before, too?

W1: Yes, but not so much. Actually, it's only since 1954, actually, that I harbour this fear in me, since, let me see, a long time now; that happened when I got married.

5.3.3 *The therapeutic effect*

Psychic symptoms manifest themselves linguistically, and at the same time psychotherapy claims to be able to treat symptoms and problems, or to re-create 'distorted language games' (Lorenzer 1973). I therefore assume that the language used by patients at the start of the therapy will be different from that used at the end. This will apply to both cognitive and emotional spheres. In the following passage the therapeutic effect is illustrated in the light of one category – the 'narrative structure' (11 main categories are used in the overall analysis: cf. Wodak 1986a).

There should typically be a predictable and significant difference in the text types of problem presentation in group therapy between solved and unsolved problems (given the same patient and the same topic). However, it should be mentioned here that only simultaneous changes at a verbal, cognitive and emotional level (expression of feelings, defence mechanisms) indicates the positive effect of the therapy.

5.3.4 *Technical aspects*

In the two texts that follow (Text A and B), the description of the non-verbal level is only an outline, and is based on the impressions of the session, which were noted down. Comments during the verbalization of the text (actions and members of the group, tone of voice) provide important additional information. The texts were transcribed using the method of Gumperz and Herasimschuk (1972) and also that of Ehlich and Switalla (HIAT) (1976: 89ff) (see Chapter 2, note 1). Each contribution, as the speaker changes is defined as a unit ('turn'). The latent levels of meaning are not recorded using linguistic categories (such as 'indirect speech act'), as the inability of speech act analysis to describe this level has already been mentioned elsewhere (Wodak 1986a). The topic of both texts exhibits one particular problem encountered by a female patient: namely the patient's extremely difficult and disturbed relationship with her parents, her father in particular. The second presentation of this problem in group therapy (Text B) was recorded exactly a year after the first (Text A), and illustrates well the change in the patient. The qualitative analysis is therefore intended not only to illustrate the technique of interpretation but also – and above all – to examine the therapeutic effect.

5.4 Text A: The problem is acute

1	F:	If there's some, well if you have a problem, you feel so
2		awful, you just wouldn't believe it (door opens, a woman
3		enters, sound of chairs being moved) and that you haven't
4		managed to cope with the problem, for example for
5		example, yes – I already said, everything's fine – last time –
6		that it was I am too calm again, although – but the
7		problem, what is inside you, what you have in you from
8		birth, or how your parents bring you up or – I don't know
9		how I should say this today, but – silly, that this is being
10		recorded, today of all days – I talked to my father, and he
11		always blames me, and after all /cough/I am only 33 years
12		old; – I can – I can't do it today
13	M:	No, finish what you were saying!
14	F:	I talk a lot, too
15	M:	Please finish!
16	F:	No, well – I know I haven't been talking for hours, but, but
17		– I haven't been through as much as him; – It's not my fault
18		that I wasn't in the war, I can't help being only as old as I
19		am and that I – that there's been no war so far. As far as we
20		are concerned, we had a family business and he reproaches
21		me that he – only yesterday we talked – I'd just like to end
22		this – we spoke on the phone – quite nicely, all calm – and
23		then like it always is – and so he accuses me, he says he
24		could have retired 10 years ago, but couldn't because I was
25		ill, you see, for 12 years I've had depressions and he never
26		lets me forget it. He says 'Yes, if you hadn't been ill, I
27		would have retired by now and would get my . . .' you
28		know, whatever he gets from his pension insurance – every
29		month. Perhaps that doesn't sound too bad, the way I tell it
30		to you, but inside me, – I can't even talk about it – I got so
31		agitated that I threw down the receiver and then he said,
32		'Yes our friends, he retired 10 years ago, the other 22 years
33		ago', – and I say don't talk rubbish, he's only – I don't
34		know – 68 years old and can't have been retired for 22
35		years. But I think I have already got that out of my head, as
36		you said last time, your father yes – I don't know – I think it
37		was you? They say you smoke such a lot and your diet, and
38		so on – he always comes to me, you see and as he says, and
39		so; I can't stand the sight of him any more, although he's
40		not bad, – he does everything for me, he has always been
41		there for me – and also I said to him once, I haven't been to
42		the doctor for 12 years and if I had a job, I'd kill my father,

43   I just can't stand it any more, this mental – I thought about
44   it, he drilled it into me for decades: 'First think, then act –
45   first think, then act, then speak', that's what I always got –
46   whenever I opened my mouth, I heard, 'first think, then act,
47   then speak'. I mean, I'm certainly not stupid, but, but – that
48   is – last year I was lucky, thank heavens, that I came to the
49   clinic, two and a half months, and I was so happy about it
50   then, and they made me better, with their medicine and I
51   thought I had got rid of it, that it had gone and for a couple
52   of months or a couple of weeks – I don't know how long,
53   these depressions have been creeping up, and now – well, I
54   can't stand it, I went to Dr . . . , and he gave me some
55   different medicine and that was fine, but – perhaps I should
56   put it like this: the person who over and over again makes
57   you go into it, why you have depressions, that you don't
58   want to see him again. – How can you do that if that
59   person is a member of your family – your own father?
60 M: Was it because of him that you got depressed, or did he?
61 F: Well, 'You'll never be able to do that, because you're too
62   stupid' – I've always had inhibitions like that, that I – if we
63   – I mean – when we went out with my husband's firm, I
64   never said a word because I was afraid to open my mouth,
65   in case I said something stupid.

1 F: *Wenn irgendein, eben so ein Problem in einem steckt, da*
2   *geht's am so, daß man glaubt, daß ma so beinander ist, daß*
3   *man gar net glaubt und daß man mit dem Problem z.B. net*
4   *fertig geworden ist, z.B. ja – ich hab g'sagt, es geht ma gut –*
5   *letztes Mal – daß es, also ich bin wieder zu ruhig, obwohl –*
6   *aber, das Problem, was in einem Menschen drinnen steckt,*
7   *daß was ma mit der Geburt mitkriegt, oder wie einen die*
8   *Eltern erzogen haben oder – I wass net, wie ich da heute*
9   *sagen soll, aber – bled, daß das gerade heute aufgenommen*
10   *wird –; i hab mit meinem Vater gesprochen, also er gibt mir*
11   *immer die Schuld, also daß ich /cough/schließlich und*
12   *endlich erst 33 Jahre alt bin; – i kann – es geht heut net.*
13 M: *No redens aus!*
14 F: *I red a viel-*
15 M: *Sprechen Sie bitte aus!*
16 F: *Na, aber – na i wass schon, daß i net a Stund jetzt red –*
17   *aber aber-daß i halt net so viel mitgemacht hab, wie er; –*
18   *daß i net im Krieg war, dafür kann i ja nix, i kann ja nix*
19   *dafür, daß i erst so alt bin und daß i bis jetzt – no ka Krieg*
20   *war, na? Oder, bei unsist es so, wir haben einen*

21 *Familienbetrieb und er hält mir eben vor, daß er – also*
22 *gestern hab'ma G'sprochen – i möcht das nur zu Ende*
23 *bringen noch – telefoniert hab'ma ganz nett, ruhig*
24 *ang'rufen – und dann ist das immer – und also, er hält mir*
25 *vor, er mant, er hätte vor 10 Jahren in Pension gehen*
26 *können, konnte aber nicht gehen, weil ich krank war, also*
27 *seit 12 Jahren die Depressionen hab und i man, des halt er*
28 *mir immer vor. Er sagt 'Ja, wenn Du net krank gewesen*
29 *wärst, da warat i schon in Pension und kriegert jedes*
30 *Monat mei' – also was er halt von der Pension kriegt, net –*
31 *vielleicht wirkt des gar net so, wenn ich das so erzähle, aber*
32 *in mir, also – kann gar net reden drüber – so hab i mi*
33 *aufg'regt, den Hörer hab hing'haut, also, und da sagt er*
34 *Äja, die Bekannten, die ma haben, der is schon 10 Jahr, der*
35 *is schon 22 Jahr' – sag i – 'erzähl ma kan Blödsinn, der is –*
36 *wass i – 68 Jahr und kann net jetzt schon 22 Jahr in*
37 *Pension – kann nicht sein'. Aber i mein, i hab des schon*
38 *abgebaut, in mir ja, so wie Sie das letzte Mal erklärt haben,*
39 *Ihr Vater net – i wass net – i glaub, Sie waren das, ja? Sie*
40 *sollen so viel rauchen und die Diät, net, also – er immer*
41 *wieder an mich heran – also, mit, wie er halt mant, also und*
42 *so; i kann ihn nit amal mehr sehen, obwohl er net schlecht*
43 *is, ja – er tut alles für mich, er war immer für mi da und – i*
44 *hab schon amal g'sagt, i bin net 12 Jahr zum Arzt 'gangen*
45 *und wenn i eing'stellt wäre, i bringert mein Vater um, i halt*
46 *des nimmer aus, das Seelische, i hab so drüber nach'denkt,*
47 *hab i von ihm – Jahrzehnte des eindrillt 'kriegt; 'Zuerst*
48 *denken, na zuerst schalten – zuerst denken schalten dann*
49 *sprechen' also, so hab i des immer – wenn i den Mund*
50 *aufg'macht hab, hab i immer 'zuerst denken, dann*
51 *schalten, dann sprechen'. I man, so dumm bin i sicher net,*
52 *aber, aber – des is – voriges Jahr hab i des Glück g'habt,*
53 *also Gott sei Dank, dass i an die Klinik 'kommen bin, 2½*
54 *Monat, und darüber war i dann so selig, und die haben*
55 *mich g'sund g'macht, mit Medikamenten und da hab i*
56 *glaubt, i hab das abgebaut, also es ist weg von mir und seit*
57 *– wass i – a paar Monat oder paar Wochen schleichen sich*
58 *langsam diese Depressionen an und jetzt – na, des halt i net*
59 *durch, war beim Herrn Dr . . . , hab – er hat mir a anderes*
60 *Mittel geben und des is ja eh gut, aber – Man sollte so*
61 *sagen: Mit dem Menschen, der einen immer wieder in das*
62 *hineintreibt, warum man ja die Depressionen hat, dass man*
63 *mit dem nie wieder in Kontakt gehen soll. – Wie kann man*

64   *denn das, wenn das so ein Mensch in der Familie is – na der*
65   *Vater?*
66 M: *Na, habens durch eahm die Depressionen 'kriegt, oder hat er?*
67 F: *Na ja, 'des kannst net, des wirst nie können, für des bist zu*
68   *bled', – bin immer schon so gehemmt gewesen, dass i –*
69   *wann ma so – wass i – mit der Firma von meinem Mann*
70   *fort'gangen san, hab i kein Wort gesprochen, weil i mi net*
71   *'traut hab, den Mund aufzumachen, dass ich vielleicht*
72   *irgendwas sag, was blöd wär.*

5.4.1 Context of the session

The patient presents her problem shortly after the commencement of the session. One has the feeling of witnessing an explosion as the problem breaks out, although she has many inhibitions about talking, particularly as the tape recorder was in sight for the first time. It is immediately obvious that the presence of the tape recorder is not subsequently a hindrance: she speaks openly and honestly, in an excited and emotional manner, about her problem. The problem is subsequently discussed almost until the end of the session, and several new aspects emerge. The interventions come mainly from a young working-class man who had described his problem with his father in the previous session and also had opened this session with a description of his dreams. The group is very emotionally involved. When the tape was played back with the therapist, the latter explained that he had allowed the problem to be discussed in such detail because many patients had troubled relationships with their parents and could therefore benefit from the discussion.

5.4.2 Colloquial level: narrative structure

The limits of quantitative evaluation are reached in the very first category (which is dealt with exclusively here). Although this is a story, the narration of a telephone call and the resulting conflicts (an 'event' in the narrative past with interspersed direct speech, in the definite personal speaker's perspective), it also includes both scenic moments (lines 44–7) and descriptions of symptoms (48–55). Classification with the aid of Labov and Waletzky's categories is fairly obvious: orientation (1–21), complication (21–35) and scenic element (44–7), evaluation (35–44), coda (resolution incorporating description of symptoms: 48–59).

Orientation: The patient begins with a description of how difficult it is to talk about her problem. She withdraws (11, 12) and continues only after encouragement (13–15), beginning with a part of the conflict: reproaches of her father (17, 18), in the face of which she justifies her actions, and a further assurance that she will not speak for too long. It is particularly interesting to note the change from the impersonal 'man' (translated as 'you') in the introduction (1, 2, 4, 6, 7, 8), with the personal interjection in 5, to the definite personal speaker's perspective 'I' in the remainder of her problem presentation.

Complication: The event (21–2) of the telephone call is not described coherently, but in brief, chopped sentences, repeatedly interrupted by the scenic description of the conflict in direct speech (reproaches of her father, self-justifications) and the description of her feelings (30).

Evaluation: Evaluation and self-reflection begin with the speech act 'I think' (35). Initially she addresses the working-class patient from whose account she appears to have learnt something. Anger and aggression then come to light, explicitly, with restrictions (39–40). The primary scene – her memory of the 'drill' – is also interwoven in the narration (44–7).

Resolution: The resolution in this case is very brief, and overlaps with both evaluation and coda. It is condensed (between 48 and 50) and changes into evaluative speech acts, disappointments, as in the coda.

Coda: She describes the conclusion of her therapeutic 'career' and again mentions the main problem: namely that it is impossible to avoid one's own father; that a solution to the conflict must be found (56–9), although this is a person who always hurts her. Part of the coda remains a description of the symptoms by the use of the descriptive present. Her explicit addressing of the therapist (54) – a sort of cry for help – is also typical.

There is a striking difference in style between complication on the one hand, and evaluation and coda on the other, from very excited, hurried and emotional speech (Feldstein *et al.* 1963, Leodolter 1975b: 260) to the assessment and to the descriptive coda, which are relatively consistent in explicit, evaluative speech acts. This is reminiscent of Labov and Fanshel's description of 'frame shifts' (1977: 35ff) (cf. 'so hab i mi aufg'regt, den Hörer hab hing'haut ... hab so drüber nach'denkt, hab i von ihm ... des eindrillt 'kriegt ... und da hab ich glaubt, ich hab das abgebaut, also es ist weg von mir

[I got so agitated that I threw down the receiver ... I thought about it, he drilled it into me ... and then I thought I had got rid of it, that it had gone]').

5.4.3 *The level of group meaning*

Text A has several functions and meanings in the transference within the group. It is not by chance that it is precisely this problem that is verbalized in the session. As mentioned above, the patient continues on from the previous session, during which a working-class patient had spoken about his relationship with his father. At the same time, she attaches her verbalization to a dream described by the same patient, and addresses him explicitly (36, 37), and is supported (13, 15) and interpreted (60) by him. There is therefore identification and solidarity between them.

The content of the father problem – the problem of authority – is not a matter of chance either. In reality the entire problem presentation should be interpreted as a censure of the therapist's authority, as disappointment that the therapy has not yet helped the patient to solve her problem. This is conclusively apparent from the coda (47ff), particularly in her direct address to the therapist (53–4). She still suffers from depression, although the doctor has prescribed medicines for her (it is possible to infer that if she didn't take them, she would kill her father) (42). Her massive feelings of guilt for taking up too much time stem on the one hand from her father's aggression towards her (11, 38, 42, 59), and on the other from her – unconscious – censure of the therapist. For this reason the coda also contains rationalizations [59].

The group gives the patient an opportunity to resolve ambivalences. To begin with, she assumes both roles in the dialogue (those of her internalized father and of herself). The former function is subsequently assumed by members of the group; the conflict with authority is acted out, but not directly against the therapist. The patient's mention of an extremely authoritarian upbringing in a scenic recollection (44–5, 45–6, 61), and the frequent repetition of reproaches (17, 18) bring out similiar associations in many members of the group. The patient's explicit mention of her fears opens her to interrogation; only several sessions later does the group discuss the sense of the therapy, certainly initiated in part by the latent disappointment of the patient.

5.4.4 The individual private linguistic level

This problem presentation in a group therapy is the patient's first major outburst in the group. She has been receiving treatment for some time, partly as an inpatient, and has been calmed by medicine. The patient's central conflict with her parents comes to light here, the difficulty of breaking away due to her massive feelings of guilt *vis-à-vis* her parents. (Only her father is mentioned in the current problem presentation. However, it subsequently becomes apparent that her mother has exemplified for her the suffering, self-sacrificing role of a woman, and so she too is involved and perhaps plays an even more important role – for example, with respect to gender identification.) Important scenes are verbalized, together with relevant feelings and connotations, and the first steps are taken towards understanding her symptoms. In spite of her inhibitions (63–5), the patient manages to describe her problem in detail, but she needs help, which she implicitly asks for (12–16). The way that she addresses other members of the group, particularly males, is typical and quite understandable as a result of her relationship with her father. Only relatively late in the course of the therapy does she also deal with women. In spite of her feelings of guilt and 'attacks on her own person', this outbreak in the group represents a great step forward. For the first time, she admits her aggression, her fantasies, her recollections of her strict father (not an unusual problem for women, though the actual experience is different and unique in each case). There is much that conforms with recent psychoanalytical concepts of women (Windoff-Héritier 1976): the bond with the therapist is very strong, and not only in this text. Her father's drill has driven her to depression; in this context she also shows a strong urge to work; she 'rushes herself', is a perfectionist (all this is subsequently mentioned in the discussion). The scenic recollection, the 'repressed language games', are very clear in this problem presentation. Lines 46 and 61–2 certainly contain specific references to the patient's father. It is only through assimilation of her past that she can come to terms with the present, and find a solution to the conflict. I can go no further into the patient's life history without compromising her anonymity.

5.5 Text B: The problem is solved

Subtext 1

```
 1  F1:  Alright, I know now, ... and I wanted to make an
 2        apppointment with Dr.......... [therapist's name] Then I
 3        only talk about my father. Now I know what's what, and
 4        what the reason is, and why he always does that, what he
 5        has done. – It's taken a long time, though.
 6  F2:  I always admire you, actually, for still working at your
 7        parents' [business]. Isn't this hard?
```

```
 1  F1:  Na ja gut. I wass ja, jetzt ... und i wollt eh mit Herrn
 2        Dr.......... an Termin ausmachen. Da red i nur über mein
 3        Vater. Jetzt wass i a, was is und was is und wieso, der
 4        Grund is warum er des immer macht, was er da g'macht
 5        hat. – Lang hat's ja dauert.
 6  F2:  I bewunder Dich eigentlich immer, dass Du immer no bei
 7        Deine Eltern arbeit'st, also. Ist das nicht schwierig?
```

Subtext 2

```
 8  F1:  Well, where should I go, something different, because deep
 9        down inside I don't have confidence that I could get a job,
10        somewhere else, full eight-hour day, and have to stand the
11        whole time, and, well, I mean, half days of course, but the
12        whole day is rather, I know, an hour during which I don't
13        do anything. But I make up for it later, as I often don't have
14        a break, or often – that's it; but going somewhere and – say
15        – working there, I'm not sure whether I – but that's not the
16        problem. I know why my father was always like that.
17  M1: I'm sorry, I don't know whether it makes you uneasy, but I
18        would like to know about it, because my situation may be
19        similar, and if you hit on something, I'd like to know what
20        you'd do then.
21  F1:  Hit on something?
22  M1: Yes.
```

```
23  F1:  Na ja, na wo soll i hingehn, was anders, weil i ma ja doch
24        irgendwie im Innersten do net zutrau, dass i wo acht
25        Stunden den ganzen Tag beschäftigt bin, ununterbrochen
26        steh und und doch, net, i man, halb tags täglich sicher, aber
27        den ganzen Tag is ja doch, dass i wass, ich a Stund, dass i
```

28   *nix tu oder so. Aber dafür hol i des dann wieder auf, dass i*
29   *oft halt ka Pause hab oder oft halt – so halt; aber aber*
30   *wohin gehen und – sag ma – dort ar – beiten, des wass i net,*
31   *ob i – aber um des gehts ja jetzt gar net. I wass, warum mei*
32   *Vater immer so war.*
33 M1: *Du, entschuldigen, i weiss net, ob's Dir so unangenehm is,*
34   *aber mich würd des aus dem Grund interessieren, weil ja so*
35   *ähnlich die Lage is veilleicht bei mir und wenn Du auf was*
36   *draufkommst, hätt i a gern g'wusst, was Du da machst.*
37 F1: *Auf was i draufkommen bin?*
38 M1: *Ja.*

Subtext 3

39 F1: Something quite harmless. You see, my father is terribly
40   jealous of me, as he's only in the workshop and doesn't do
41   anything else and I and mother actually do everything, you
42   see, the business and everything, you know. That's bad
43   luck, when the old man is no longer able to do everything. I
44   mean, I accept it. He is 70, and his achievements in life
45   were when he was young, and now he can't manage any
46   more, and when he comes into the workshop, he says,
47   'there now, another repair for 1,500, – another 3,000, –',
48   and if you count it, that makes three repairs for 90, –
49   Schillings you know, and he says S 1,500, –. Well, you don't
50   say anything and because he has got the customers . . . and
51   so on. Mother always says 'my word', it's too much for her
52   and this and that and now for days he has been so angry
53   and so cross and so aggressive towards me and he was like
54   that toward me again last Friday, you see; but, thank
55   heavens it wasn't so bad that I collapsed at work, you see. I
56   was just a bit, I was unsteady, and I thought, 'My God, if I
57   fall so low again, how will I ever get up again,' you see. But
58   I did – three days later it was all over and forgotten, you
59   see. And at night he laughed again and said, 'Look, it hurts
60   me, because I shout at you and get excited, it doesn't hurt
61   you so much. I suffer, not you.' /laughs/ So I'd have to
62 M2: I think, both parties suffer in a quarrel like that!
63 F1: Yes, well it's all the same to me now.
64 M1: But it's nice if you know the relationships.
65 F1: Yes, of course, once you know.

66   F1: *Auf eh ganz was harmloses. Also mei Vater is furchtbar*
67   *eifersüchtig auf mi, und dass er halt nur in der Werkstatt*
68   *isund sunst nix tut und i eigentlich mit der Mutter alles*
69   *mach, net, das G'schäft und des alles, net. Des is halt a, is*
70   *halt a Pech, wann der Chef nimmermehr halt so kann. I*
71   *man, I sehs ja ein. Er ist 70, er hat halt in seinen früheren*
72   *Jahren des geleistet, und jetzt gehts halt nimmer, net und*
73   *wann er in die Werkstatt kommt, sagt er, 'da, schon wieder*
74   *1,500, – Reparatur, scho wieder 3,000, –' und wann das*
75   *zählst, sans drei Reparaturen um 90, – S net, und sagen tut*
76   *er 1,500, – net. Na, da redst halt nix und, weil er hat die*
77   *Kunden … und so. Die Mutti erzählt immer 'na Jessasna',*
78   *s'is ihr scho zuviel und des tuts und des machts und jetzt,*
79   *san da, seit Tagen hat er so einen Zorn und eine Wut und*
80   *eine Aggression auf mich g'habt und die hat er mir dann*
81   *halt vorigen Freitag wieder spüren lassen, net; aber es is,*
82   *Gott sei Dank, nimmermehr so tief gegangen, dass i im*
83   *Betrieb umg'fallen bin, net. I war nur a bissl halt, war i*
84   *unsicher, hab i ma 'denkt, 'Jesas-Maria, wenn i jetzt wieder*
85   *tiefer g'fallen bin, wie komm i da wieder auf', net. Aber i*
86   *bin – nach drei Tag wars wieder vorbei und vergessen, net.*
87   *Und er hat auf'd Nacht schon wider g'lacht und hat g'sagt,*
88   *Schau, weh tuts mir ja, weil i schrei mit Dir und i reg mi*
89   *auf, Dir tut ja des gar net so weh, i leid ja und net Du'.*
90   */laughs/. Also müsste*
91   M2: *ich glaub, beide leiden bei so an Streit.*
92   F1: *Ja, des is ma jetzt scho egal.*
93   M1: *Es is angenehm, wenn ma's weiss, net, die*
94   *Zusammenhänge.*
95   F1: *Na ja sicher, wenn ma einmal weiss.*

5.5.1 Context of the session

This session focused on the job problem. Several patients had described their difficulties in detail, in particular a middle-class male patient, a civil servant. Even the therapist intervened, pointing out how the latter tended to go round in circles. The other patients in the group were bored, I noticed that our middle-class female patient (this session was recorded exactly a year later) wanted to say something. She began by addressing the therapist directly, and announced that she had actually discovered the solution to a problem.

5.5.2 Selection of the text

A problematic sequence of discourse has been chosen here deliberately: it consists of three problem presentations (by formal definition) that together make up one problem presentation, in view of the fact that subtexts 1 and 2 can be regarded as introductions to subtext 3, which contains both an account and a problem solution. This is the knowledge acquired by the patient, which has enabled her to see things in a different perspective. This type of immanently coherent problem presentation in group therapy must be regarded as something of an exception, and was selected for interpretation with this in mind. Most problem presentations in group therapy are not complete, the problem continues to be dealt with after verbalization.

The limits of quantification are thus particularly clear in this instance. Three problem presentations have to be classified from the necessarily restrictive definition of the contribution to the discussion (determined by change of speaker), although intrinsically and thematically the texts belong together. It is thus difficult to assign them to categories, because all three types of text occur. Subtexts 1 and 2 are descriptions of circumstances; in subtext 3 an 'event' with scenic elements is interwoven in the problem solution. However, in text 3 in particular, the value of the story is of secondary importance.

Subtext 1 (1–7) can be assigned to the category of 'circumstance', although it contains a definite speaker's perspective, an active voice and factual mood, which point rather to 'scene' and 'narration'. Subtext 2 (8–22) can definitely be assigned to the category of 'circumstance'. The description of everyday life at work is passive. However, it must be regarded as a strategy of justification, as an answer to the implicit reproach in lines 6, 7. As far as interpretation is concerned, subtext 3 is a 'parable': a small story illustrates the nature of the problem solution, representing this and the newly acquired strategies for coping with the conflict. It must therefore be assumed that this is a mixed type (with regard to narrative structure). Circumstance (problem solution) and narration are interwoven and occur simultaneously.

The success of the therapy is thus manifest not only in the content of the successful problem solution, but also in the form, in a new type of text which contains elements of all three basic types:

circumstantial, scenic and narrative elements occur without special priority being given to any one component, a **mixed type of problem presentation.**

In the context of the session and its group dynamics, subtexts 1 and 2 pave the way for subtext 3 (and can be interpreted as strategies for awakening curiosity). Subtext 3 is therefore mainly used in the qualitative analysis, as an example of the effect of therapy on the form of problem presentation in group therapy.

5.5.3 Colloquial level: narrative structure

The problematics of this classification (**see below**) have already been mentioned: first, subtext 2 contains an introduction to a circumstantial description, which is rudely interrupted in line 16. Secondly, the core of the problem presentations is the problem solution (39–51), with a narration inserted by way of illustration. Lastly, the resolution follows (59–61). The text was classified as a 'mixed type' mainly for psychoanalytical reasons, after playback with the therapist. The patient is naturally concerned about the renewed conflict with her father, but is now in a position to relate it differently, against the background of a problem solution.

Psychoanalytically, the question remains as to whether the suggested problem solution can be considered a rationalization, thus only a purely intellectual solution of the problem. Such an interpretation is strengthened by the patient's subsequent reluctance to admit that she suffers in the conflict, though she certainly must. On the other hand, the validity of the problem solution is strongly supported by other factors, by the patient's distance to her problem – both discursively and emotionally – and by her new, and different way of coping with the conflict. An interpretation of the text as rationalization is also refuted by the strong emotional involvement. As is so often the case in therapeutic communication, various motives and interpretations can be initially applied, many of them conflicting. Only subsequent conversations with the patient would allow for a definite reading.

> **Introduction:** The introduction is particularly long (1–5, 8–16, 39). The patient begins twice, mainly because the intervention in line 6 forces her briefly into a circumstantial description, which is also related in another linguistic style. Conflict and ambivalence can be felt here (short, incomplete sentences, pauses, hesitations, expletives).

She announces her knowledge of her problem, makes the group curious by saying that it is only the therapist she wants to tell about her insight. Text 2 is thus a renewed description of everyday life at work, presented as a justification of the internalized (and not explicitly verbalized) reproach of her father that she does not work enough. However, it follows the intervention, which she obviously misinterprets (perceiving it as a reproach instead of praise). Only the intervention (17–20) induces the patient to describe her solution.

Problem solution: 39–53 must be classified as an evaluation, a metacommunicative, reflexive speech act (strategies for problem solution are metacommunicative acts). The patient interprets the conflict and sets the frame in which the 'event', the complication, must be seen. It is this consistent, calmly presented evaluation in particular that indicates the speaker's new perspective. The linguistic style is significantly different from that used in subtext 2 and text A. She outlines her father, and has a better understanding of him.

Narration: The actual incident comes to light only in 39–58, an incident (she almost collapsed) which is dealt with briefly. The speaker merely mentions the incident in a subordinate clause (54–5: 'dass i im Betrieb umg'fallen bin [that I collapsed at work]'). The speaker relates feelings and reactions, and how she copes with the conflict (55–7): this is again evaluative. Although the incident was certainly a terrible one for her, her language remains consistent here (there is a definite personal speaker's perspective – she is excited – but significantly different from that in text A).

Resolution: The summary of the problem presentation is partly narrative, partly evaluative and reflective. The patient describes her strategy for coping with the conflict, and at the same time she assesses her condition, expressing pleasure at her successful strategy. A scenic moment is also woven in, as a sort of conclusion (59–61). This is her father's realization (and her own) that he is actually the one who suffers most from this conflict.

5.5.4 The level of group meaning

This problem presentation is particularly interesting with regard to group dynamics. The patient wishes to describe her success to the group, and to be praised (the kind of expectations that are otherwise directed at the family). At the same time, she wants to make the group curious, even jealous, by initially addressing the therapist directly (2). She has 'made it', while others have not. The group immediately takes its revenge in the intervention in line 6: the hidden problems that the patient did not want to mention come to light. The group reproaches her with not having solved her job problem – so she need not think she is any better, or possibly loved more by the therapist. One can feel the terrible dread that somebody could be better off than oneself, could be more advanced in the therapy. The competition, even for the therapist (the female patient who intervenes is very dependent on the therapist (6, 7)), can therefore be regarded as a justification, laden with feelings of guilt even *vis-à-vis* the group. The intervention in line 17, in which a male patient shows interest, helps the patient to drop the unpleasant subject and express solidarity and a willingness to learn. The male patient in particular is pleased to have his problem dealt with by others, so that he can act as listener and interpreter, a role which he also assumes here. Praise for the account is not immediately forthcoming, whereupon the female patient withdraws, disappointed. She has not received what she wanted: the group has not behaved as she, unrealistically, had expected it to. Nobody likes to see success. It is clear that the mechanisms in the group are similiar to those in everyday life. The patient subsequently assimilates her disappointment, and in doing so acquires a slightly more realistic viewpoint.

5.5.5 *The individual private linguistic level*

For the first time the patient is able to feel pleasure and happiness, to feel pleased at her success. The terrible ambivalence and the conflict situation have been cleared up; she can now see things in perspective and is better able to cope with any conflicts that may arise. She also dares to admit her pleasure publicly, something which she was previously unable to do, in keeping with her socially imposed, suffering female role. The fact that she is still unstable is shown by her rapid retreat after the intervention in line 6, her regressive tendencies (51, 52) and her great disappointment (63) when praise is not forthcoming. She can now tackle her problems, above all her job problem and her relationship with her mother, on the basis of her new perspective, her first resolution of a conflict. The entire narrative mode has changed (as shown by the linguistic indicators): she describes the strategy used to solve her problem self-confidently and coherently. There is also a far higher degree of explicit, verbalized self-reflection. She is no longer torn between different evaluations: she has found her own standard, establishes her own evaluative frame, puts forward arguments and explanations. The difference from text A is obvious, providing evidence of the effect of the therapy, which is linguistically apparent ('mixed type'). This patient cannot be regarded as cured, but her progress is unmistakable, her renewed pleasure in life which finds expression in this 'joyous outcry':

> You're so glad you've made it, that you, that you realize how happy you are, and I have to say, my God, the beautiful, well, the day is beautiful and – excuse me if I just say this quickly – I have such a wonderful view from my living room, I look out into the woods and now – when I was just feeling so happy and my father says – 'no work to do' –. Well, just for a moment I – I didn't quite realize what he had said, I was so intent on the view. My husband immediately looked at me, 'Please don't say anything, please, otherwise there'll be trouble again' – But inside me, I really needed that, such things; life is wonderful, life is worth living!
>
> *Man freut sich so, dass man es geschafft hat, dass man, dass man sieht, dass man glücklich ist, und ich muss sagen, mein Gott, der schöne, also der Tag ist schön und – entschuldigen, dass i des no gschwind dazu sag, – i hab so ein' herrlichen Blick vom Wohnzimmer, i siech im Wald rauf und jetzt – und wie i grad so glücklich war und mei Vater sagt drauf – 'nichts zu arbeiten' – Also momentan hab i ma – hab i des gar net so mit'kriegt, weil i so in die Gegend 'schaut hab. Mein Mann hat mi sofort ang'schaut, 'Bitte sag nix, bitte, sonst is wieder was' – Aber in mir drinnen, des hab i wieder notwenig g'habt, so Sachen; das Leben, wie schön, das Leben ist lebenswert!*

5.6 Final remarks

Although a single qualitative text analysis can only succeed in illustrating the hypotheses, I believe that it does demonstrate the sense of applying linguistic indicators to an investigation of the therapeutic effect. This positive impression was strengthened and further evidenced by case studies and interviews carried out in the course of the overall investigation (Wodak 1986a).

This is not a 'superficial' change (a new type of text being introduced, as it were), but a deep and lasting alteration of personality. To this extent it can be said that the occurrence of the 'mixed-type', coupled with changes at the emotional and cognitive level, can be regarded as indicators of the positive effect of therapy.

Coming back to the question of the consequences of more

verbalization and communication, we have to conclude that therapeutic discourse, due to its specific setting, the therapeutic technique applied and its isolation from everyday life, allows for small steps towards emancipation. In this case, as in others, the behaviour of the patient changes drastically, and she is able to cope with her life in a more satisfactory way. Through an analysis of the power relationship to the therapist, the patient finally arrives at her core problem: the authority of her father. Learning to deal with this troubling relationship enables her to come to terms with other power relationships that she is involved in. Thus, power, in this specific context, is not mystified but made explicit and thus refutable.

Notes

1. See Wodak (1986a) for an overview, Lakoff (1992) and Cederborg (1994) for an analysis of psychoanalytic and family therapy sessions.
2. The first time I employed this methodology was in the study of courtroom interaction (Leodolter 1975a) which I have not included in this book for obvious reasons: the data are old, and much has changed in the structure and process of court trials. Also, the main analysis in the study of courtroom interaction focused on the level of phonology, discourse sequences were only used as illustrative evidence. Nevertheless, this study triggered all the following research and established the grounds of the methodology and experience with fieldwork.
3. The significant differences compared with everyday conversation and the explicit underlying rules of discourse are spelled out in Wodak (1986a). It is important to mention three rules here:

   'Say everything that comes into your mind'
   'Listen to others speaking'
   'Observe the communication process and talk about it as well'.

   There is no space here to go into details about the psychotherapeutic techniques. But again, it seems to be relevant to mention two basic assumptions: it is assumed that an unconscious (*Unbewußtes, ES*) exists, and thus becomes manifest in the free associating discourse. One goal of therapy is to make the unconscious conscious, thus allowing the patient to uncover repressed feelings, situations, desires and fears. Secondly, the concept of transference is important. Psychotherapists assume that everybody projects experiences and feelings from earlier relationships (mostly to primary caretakers) into new relationships, thus distorting them. Therapy should uncover these distortions, thus making it possible to constrict one's own relationships consciously (see Wodak 1986a for further details).

4. The tape recordings were transcribed with HIAT (see Chapter 2, note 1). I decided that these illustrative problem presentations should be more accessible to readers, and thus transferred them – in the translation from German to English – into an understandable colloquial style. Repetitions etc. are not edited out. The authentic transcriptions can be found in the German book (Wodak 1981a, b).

6 Conclusion

The picture of the **disordered discourses** described in the preceding chapters is certainly not an overly optimistic one: in institutions as well as in everyday life, we are continuously confronted with various kinds of such disorders. These are in no way random or chaotic; they possess their own order and serve certain functions of exclusion, power, justification and legitimation. They manifest and reproduce certain interests of the elites in our societies, interests which differ from context to context and situation to situation.

6.1 The normality of chaos

In doctor–patient interaction in the outpatient clinics we have investigated, discursive disorders establish certain routines and justify the actions of the powerful. Doctors exercise power over their patients, they ask the questions, they interrupt and introduce new topics, they control the conversation. Patients are expected to comply with the explicit and implicit norms of the clinic procedures. From this perspective, ideal patients would be those who have experience, know the jargon, can explain their symptoms in technical language, reply with precise and short answers and do not expect the doctors to listen to their stories from everyday life. They should trust the doctors completely and not ask 'unnecessary' questions. The manifest function of the interaction between doctor and patient is to arrive at a diagnosis as quickly as possible, as time is extremely valuable. Doctors always seem to be in a rush, to be extremely busy and to exude a sense of overburdened agitation.

Such patients are, of course, rare, and the normal course of events is correspondingly different: Some patients come with no experience of medical examinations; a few are not aware that they might have to undress in front of the doctors. The doctors themselves some-times do not have enough expertise to make a diagnosis or prescribe a remedy, and have to wait for the senior consultant. Data and documents get lost or mixed up. The equipment may not work as well as expected, and some tests have to be repeated. The doctors – who are often on duty for more than 30 hours at a time – are sometimes exhausted. Outpatient clinics, moreover, are usually staffed by inexperienced doctors though more experienced person-nel could cope better with the volume of patients and range of symptoms. The outpatient clinic is viewed as a field for learning, and is a relatively low prestige assignment. More prominent patients or those paying privately are dealt with by university teaching physicians and senior consultants anyway. Inequality on all levels is apparent and is continously reinforced.

The hierarchy inside the hospital exposes the young doctors who staff the outpatient clinics to many pressures. Owing to the values and myths of the institution, they are expected to live up to the image of omniscience, although they are actually in training. Their roles require them to exercise, and embody, authority when they do not have the corresponding expertise. In many situations, it is the nurses who often will have worked in the clinic for years, who possess the requisite knowledge; yet they are required to package their greater expertise in a way that does not threaten the doctor's overall authority. The young doctors are also subjected to super-vision by the senior doctors, who often enough revise decisions made initially. Misunderstandings of all kinds also occur constantly. To cite but one example: doctors confer about the condition of the previous patient while another patient is waiting to be examined; this latter patient gets more and more nervous because he or she does not realize that the conversation is about someone else. Again, it takes time to clear up such a misunderstanding.

In the study of the Vienna outpatient clinic and in our example in Chapter 2, an unexpected event completely disrupted the routine: the doctors needed to remove their cars from the parking lot. One such event triggered a whole chain of other events; the already very unstable structure breaks down. Doctors are not able and not trained to deal with surprises and unexpected events. Total disorder is the consequence.

The use of ethnographic and discourse sociolinguistic methods to study the outpatient clinic enabled us to uncover the many different functions and myths of this particular institutional culture. In contrast to much other research, we did not seek to find a 'guilty' party. The picture is not a dichotomous one, where clearly the outsiders are the goodies and the insiders the baddies. The systematic disorders lie much deeper and are not caused by some single individual. Does this mean that no changes are possible without revamping the whole structure of this institution? In this case, no. Agents within the institutional structure (both insiders and outsiders) who merely act in a more critically reflective way would make a significant difference: patients who do not hesitate to ask questions, and doctors who listen and are conscious of the relationship developing between the patient and themselves. A holistic approach – back to the human being and away from 'the broken foot' or 'the lung' – would change the discourses in a qualitative way. In a programme developed for doctors (Lalouschek *et al.* 1987) we drafted guidelines for conscientious doctors and patients that were successfully applied in training young doctors. Even such small steps mean that some myths have to be dismantled: doctors, for example, should be able to confess that they do not know everything without losing their authority as experts. Most importantly, these changes in discourse do not need more time, the time is just used differently. Critical linguistics, within the domain of medicine, may thus have an emancipatory impact on all parties involved.

6.2 The pyramid of power

In recent years, schools have come under considerable pressure because of the influx of immigrants and refugees, and have come under increasing criticism in the media and in public areas. Since the fall of the Iron Curtain in 1989 and the beginning of the war in Bosnia the percentage of children enrolled whose native language is not German has risen to 60% or 80% in some Viennese schools. Yet neither teachers nor curricula were prepared for these new developments. Many Austrians also complain that schools end at lunch time. Parents (i.e. mothers) are expected to pick up their children and take care of them at home. Day-care centres do exist, but tend to be organized in a very formal and dull way. These are only a few examples of problems that have become the focus of attention recently.

In response to earlier similar concerns, a school partnership, which was to allow schools to become more democratic and transparent, was established by statute. A range of different committees was created at which organizational and curricular problems are debated and measures adapted. Teachers, pupils and parents all participate in these various meetings. The chairperson is elected, the agenda of the meeting is supposed to be circulated in advance and be adopted by the committee members. The aim of the school partnership is to ensure participation in the decison-making process in the schools, and to ensure certain legal rights of teachers, parents and pupils. Despite these reforms, Austrian schools continue to be characterized by a very rigid hierarchy. Principals make the decisions inside the school, but are forced to defend these decisions before the Ministry of Education. Teachers are superintended by the principals, and pupils subject to the control of both. Inside the schools, then, power is explicitly defined and hierarchically organized. Parents remain outside this explicit power structure: they are needed in several ways, as fundraisers, but also as scapegoats – because problem pupils are always consigned to their mothers (sic) (the school rarely sees itself as a cause of the problems). Thus, parents are not systematically integrated.

The study of the school partnership which employed ethnographic as well as discourse sociolinguistic methods was commissioned by the Ministry of Education itself. Officials wanted to know what kind of impact the law had had at various types of school. In other words, had the schools achieved the democratic promise held out by the school partnership laws? Our findings did not bear out the officials' hopes. We demonstrated that the implementation of the law had not actually altered the previous hierarchy and dependencies in the schools. The possibilities which the law actually provided for were not used, no substantial debates and discussions occurred at the meetings, nearly every motion was approved unanimously, and questions at meetings concerned only organizational details. The headteachers were usually elected as chairpersons of committees, which only increased their power. In the committees where parents became chairs, the headteachers were still present and took up most of the available discourse space. Even tenured teachers did not dare or did not want to participate in the discussions. When we interviewed some of them about their silence, the general answers were that 'it does not make sense', 'nothing has changed', 'decisions are taken elsewhere' (in the principal's office, in the ministries), or 'we do not want conflicts'. This suggests one important myth about the school: the institution is harmonious, 'everybody is in the same boat', no conflicts should occur. The teachers resigned themselves to their passive roles; they did not appear to believe that they could possibly play an active role.

After reviewing the results, we made several suggestions for change which would promote more substantive democratic activity. For example, information should be complete and made available to everyone; the chair should be someone other than the head-teacher; these chairpersons should be able to take part and observe, but certainly should not be entitled to dominate the time allotted for discussion. Adequate time should be set aside for meetings so that time pressures would not inhibit participation or the democratic procedures. Agendas should be sent out two weeks beforehand so that everybody is able to prepare for the meetings. Most importantly, all participants should be informed of their rights under the partnership laws and should be encouraged to practise active discussion behaviour. Parents and pupils need to be reassured that they would not face negative sanctions if they disagreed with the school administration. Finally, and importantly, if issues concerning the curricula and other relevant substantive problems were actually discussed in such meetings, they would lose their token function.

Our study of the school partnership illustrated the limits of critical linguistic research in two ways: a change of discourse alone does not necessarily reflect, or translate into, a modification of power relationships. In the case we studied, in fact, a change of discourse meant a mystification of actual power: the meetings really assumed a perfunctory quality, which reinforced the appearance, rather than the substance of participation. A kind of pseudo-democratization had taken place which obscured the strong and rigid hierarchy. Success in such endeavours would thus seem to depend not only upon changes of discourse, but also upon changes in the attitudes of agents and in the structures of the institution.

At the same time, the officials who had commissioned the study were displeased with its results. Assuming that the study would confirm the positive image they had of the partnership, these officials had hoped to exploit the results of this study in the media and, perhaps, to enhance the image of politicians who authored the legislation. When confronted with the results, and with the researchers' unwillingness to alter them to fit the officials' preferred outcome, they seemed to project their anger about the institutional structure itself onto the researchers, accusing them of having falsified both data and results. This particular conflict between the scholarly integrity of critical researchers and the officials more attuned to the exigencies of political public relations has not been resolved to this very day.

6.3 'What's new?'

Disorders in discourse do not only occur within institutions, between insiders and outsiders or within the hierarchy itself. They also appear outside of the institution. All institutions produce information which is relevant to those outside.

In democratic societies, people are supposed to participate in decision-making, and elect their representatives. In order to carry out these responsibilities they need to be informed. Mindful of this model of democratic citizenship, the Austrian Radio Broadcasting Company like its British counterpart, the BBC, is required to observe certain rules of objectivity regarding the views presented, and to ensure the comprehensibility of the material as a whole. Regular radio news broadcasts briefly (in the case studied, five minutes) summarize the most important events of the day. These news items are intended to serve as basic information for the public. The public depends on such news broadcasts for a variety of reasons. Many people switch on the radio first thing in the morning, either wanting to know if everything is still all right in their small world, or with more specific aims such as: Who won the election? What happened in X? etc. Many informants in the study stated that they felt more secure if they understood what was happening in the world. Older people particularly often rely on the radio. Other people have different listening habits: to some, the radio serves as background noise, while working, others at home feel less lonely when the radio is on. A large part of our sample did not read newspapers, and thus relied on the radio as its sole source of information.

Our study of the comprehension and comprehensibility of news broadcasts showed that up to 70% of those who listen to these broadcasts do not completely understand them. Certain items, especially so-called 'quote stories' are particularly difficult to comprehend if the necessary background knowledge is missing. For example, if you do not know how the war in Bosnia has broadly developed, small information units are difficult to digest and update their existing knowledge. But a lack of education is not the sole cause of misunderstanding or non-understanding. People who are very angry at party politics are hindered in their understanding of a news item by their emotional reaction, often triggered by one specific word. They start to associate an item with their own life experiences and debate with the news. This affects their listening attentiveness: such listeners hear only what they expect to hear or what reinforces their opinions and prejudices. Feelings of help-lessness are also demotivating. As wars go on and politicians do not find solutions or even make peace, people begin to feel desperate and powerless, and resist hearing more about such terrible things. They do not want disorder in the world.

However, the content of news items is only part of the difficulty. The linguistic form of the radio news broadcasts tends to be confusing. Nominalizations, abstractions, strange and arcane words, passive constructions, implicit argumentation structures, etc. form barriers to understanding. Thus, the texts are a primary cause of disorders in discourse. The fact that written language is produced for oral reception is a paradox, as the way we speak is very different from the way we write. On the other hand, when asked if they would prefer news in vernacular, many informants said no – the news broadcasts would lose their authority if they adopted colloquial speech. People thus seem to be more reassured if the news still sounds important and official, even if they do not understand it. Class and gender also play a role in the differential understanding of the news. The better-educated understand more of the content, while women tend to understand some topics better than men and vice versa, which might reflect the respective interests in different issues.

We tested listeners' comprehension of various versions of refor-mulated news broadcasts. In one version, the text was simplified, in the second the text coherence was altered qualitatively. But both versions were the same length as the original broadcast and were spoken by the same newsreaders. We tested these reformulations, and the results again show the limits of critical research. The better-educated understood the revised news broadcasts much better, i.e. they became better informed, while the less-educated understood somewhat more, but the gap between these groups widened rather than narrowed. In the final analysis, improving a news broadcast's comprehensibility disproportionately benefited the educational elites. The greater part of the population is even more excluded from daily information and thus from active participation in a democratic society. Thus, linguistic reformulations must be augmented by more extensive background information as well as detailed knowledge about politics. People also need to be trained to listen to news more sceptically: understanding how certain topics are included or excluded from the news, for example, requires some knowledge about the news production process.

The studies involving the intersection of institution and everyday life were designed differently from those investigating the 'endogenously' institutional cultures themselves. In the former case, ethnographic information was used in a non-systematic way, tests on text comprehension were standardized and many informants were interviewed. In interpreting the results, we had to take the test situation into account. As many informants had the feeling that they were being examined and were frightened, we needed to reassure them that we were actually investigating the incomprehensibility of texts and not their knowledge. More studies in this area are needed which would provide a more systematic ethnographic perspective, for example, watching and taping people actually listening to the news at home. On the other hand, the more formal and restrictive methodologies employed in the studies cited provided comparable quantitative results: we were able to demonstrate that the same discourses are understood very differently by specific groups of informants, and we could also test the reformulations. The model of text comprehension which was a product of these investigations integrates the cyclical process of understanding on both the cognitive and the emotional levels.

Critical linguistics, therefore, can make differences in comprehension apparent, while a discourse analysis of texts can clarify the disorders inherent in the given discourse. But critical linguistics as such can not change the inequalities in information reception. Education of the users is necessary and training in critical reflection of official information is needed as well. These are tasks for the future, and not only for critical linguists.

6.4 Therapeutic discourse: a model for change?

Chapter 5 presented the results of a longitudinal study of language behaviour in group therapy. This, too, was an ethnographic study of an institutional culture and discourse which observe very different rules from those which obtain in everyday life. The therapeutic group for suicidal patients that formed the focus of the study is located in a crisis intervention centre. The aim of the therapists and social workers in this centre is to help severely depressed and disturbed people in coping with their existential problems. As a consequence, the discourse within the institution itself is very different from those of the other institutions we studied. All the insiders have been forced to confront very depressing aspects of our society, and those dealing therapeutically with patients had their own supervised 'metatherapy' sessions for discussing their own problems related to their work. A hierarchy naturally exists, with the director of the centre in a dominant position *vis-à-vis* all others, and the specialized therapists in a position of relative dominance *vis-à-vis* the social workers. Nevertheless, conflicts which arise are not swept under the carpet, but are discussed openly. Team sessions are frequently taken up with lengthy debates about the work at the centre.

The therapeutic group met every weekday, but it was an open group, with new members both welcome and common. Suicidal patients thus had a place to go to every day. The group also met outside of the therapeutic environment: they had dinner together, organized Christmas festivities, etc. Often, people who met at the group became close friends. The rules in the group contrast strongly with those of everyday life: you are encouraged to say everything that comes into your head; arguments and conflicts are welcome; you are expected to listen to the problems of others and try to offer advice. Participants are also urged to reflect on the group discussion as such; routine forms of politeness, for example, are not considered necessary; emotions may be shown. These explicit rules are explained to every newcomer and have an immediate effect on the discourse: misunderstandings, conflicts, disorders of all kinds are explicitly integrated into the conversation and are resolved. Very intimate topics are dealt with at length, and everyone gets their turn. Very few speakers are interrupted. After two years spent observing this group, many changes in the patients became apparent. In contrast to some previous influential studies, we found that work-ing-class members were able to adapt to this discourse context, and could also articulate their problems and feelings. Class-specific and gender-specific differences in discourse production emerged, but despite these, everyone was helped. 'Problem presentations' were a preferred approach of the group, and three different types evolved: a scenic problem presentation, a narrative and a circumstantial description. These types were also significantly distributed, both working-class men and women tended to utter scenic problem presentations, middle-class women narrated their experiences, and middle-class men described their symptoms. Changes in psycho-dynamics manifested themselves in the changes of discourse types: a mixed type evolved, which contained elements of all three basic forms, and provided a solution to a problem that was both cognitively and emotionally satisfactory.

The erection of class or gender barriers was vigilantly counter-acted; and if it was felt that they had surfaced, they were discussed immediately. This kind of discourse recalls Habermas' utopian vision of the ideal speech situation (see 1.5.2 above). The discourse in this therapeutic situation promotes and reinforces self-reflection. Moreover, changes occur in the group discussion process as a whole as well as in the individuals. These are not just superficial changes or discourse reformulations, but changes of action, changes of entire language-games. Interviews conducted with the patients in their homes after their therapy showed how much had actually changed in a positive way for them. Many had started new lives, had formed new relationships, had begun new jobs, or had come to terms with their former life in a qualitatively new way. In a word, they had become active agents who had started to alter those circumstances which they were in a position to influence them-selves, and in the end became flexible enough to provide themselves with some happiness. In this case, discourse in this very specific setting had an emancipatory effect.

What does this imply for a critical discourse sociolinguistics? Are we to adapt the model of the therapeutic situation for everyday life and for institutions? In some ways, this is already being done: experts on organization advise institutions, and such institutions frequently work more efficiently afterwards than they did before-hand. But the aim of critical discourse sociolinguistics cannot be merely to make people feel happy, or to help them adapt and work more efficiently in an institution without questioning its underlying power structure. Such an outcome would be tantamount to achieving what Bourdieu called 'symbolic violence' (Bourdieu 1987), i.e. the perfect acceptance of inequality and power. The aim of critical discourse sociolinguistics is, on the contrary, to assist and advance reflection: to promote critical agents who query the underlying assumptions of structures in our society and equip them with the linguistic tools for demystifying power relationships, and deharmonizing pseudo-harmony. Some rules of therapeutic discourse could, indeed should, be transferred to everyday life situations. People ought finally to accept conflicts and contradictions, in short, disorders, as part of the human condition. For only if we do so can we expect to change the structures and the power relations which define them.

Bibliography

Ammon U, Dittmar N, Mattheier K (eds) 1987 *Sociolinguistics – Soziolinguistik* De Gruyter, Amsterdam

Angus L E 1992 Metaphor and the communication interaction in psychotherapy: a multimethodological approach. In S H Toukmanian, D L Rennie (eds) *Psychotherapy Process Research: Paradigmatic and Narrative Approaches* Sage, Newbury Park, CA: 187–210

Antos G, Augst G (eds) 1989 *Textoptimierung* Huber, Bern

Archibald K A 1976 Drei Ansichten über die Rolle des Experten im politischen Entscheidungsprozess: Systemanalyse, Inkrementalismus und klinischer Ansatz. In B Badura (ed) *Seminar: Angewandte Sozialforschung* Suhrkamp, Frankfurt: 187–204

Ballstaedt S *et al.* 1981a *Texte verstehen – Texte gestalten* Fink, München

Ballstaedt S *et al.* 1981b Zur Vorhersagbarkeit von Lernergebnissen auf der Basis hierarchischer Textstrukturen. In E Mandl (ed) 1981 *Zur Psychologie der Textverarbeitung* Fink, München

Barthes R 1974 *Mythen des Alltags* Suhrkamp, Frankfurt

Bartlett F 1932 *Remembering. A study in Experimental and Social Psychology* Cambridge University Press

Beaugrande R 1994 *Studies in Critical Discourse Analysis* Longman

Beaugrande R, Dressler W 1981 *Einführung in die Textlinguistik* Niemeyer, Tübingen

Becker-Mrotzek M 1991 Kommunikation und Sprache in Institutionen. Ein Forschungsbericht zur Analyse institutioneller Kommunikation. Teil II: Arbeiten zur Kommunikation in juristischen Institutionen. *Deutsche Sprache* 19/4: 350–72

Bell A 1991 *The Language of News Media* Blackwell

Benke G 1994 Journalistenfreiräume: eine textlinguistische Untersuchung von Nachrichtenagenturtexten und ihrer Verwendung in zwei Österreichischen Zeitungen. MA thesis, University of Vienna

Bennet A E (ed) 1985 *Communication between Doctors and Patients* Oxford University Press

Bernstein B (ed) 1970 *Soziale Struktur, Sozialisation und Sprachverhalten* De Munter, Amsterdam

Bion W R 1961 *Experiences in Groups* Tavistock

Bliesener T 1982 *Die Visite – ein verhinderter Dialog* Narr, Tübingen

Boden D, Zimmerman D H (eds) 1993 *Talk and Social Structure* Polity Press

Bourdieu P 1979 *Entwurf einer Theorie der Praxis* trans. C. Pialoux. Suhrkamp, Frankfurt

Bourdieu P 1987 *Die Kritik der feinen Unterschiede* Suhrkamp, Frankfurt

Brown G, Yule G 1985 *Discourse Analysis* Cambridge University Press

Brown R, Gilman A 1968 The pronouns of power and solidarity. In J Fishman (ed) 1968 *Readings in the Sociology of Language* Mouton, The Hague: 252–76

Brünner G, Graefen G (eds) 1993a *Texte und Diskurse* Westdeutscher Verlag, Opladen

Brünner G, Graefen G 1993b Einleitung: zur Konzeption der funktionalen Pragmatik. In Brünner/Graefen (eds) 1993a: 7–24

Buttny R, Cohen J R 1991 The uses of goals in therapy. In K Tracy *Understanding Face-to-Face Interaction: Issues Linking Goals and Discourse* Lawrence Erlbaum Associates, Hillsdale, NJ: 63–77

Cederborg A-C 1994 Family Therapy as collaborative work. PhD thesis, Linköping University

Cicourel A V 1981 Language and medicine. In C Ferguson, S Heath (eds) 1981: 403–30

Cicourel A V 1985 Doctor–Patient discourse. In van Dijk 1985 (Vol. 4): 193–202

Cicourel A V 1987 Cognitive and organizational aspects of medical diagnostic reasoning *Discourse Processes* 10: 347–67

Cicourel A V 1992 The interpenetration of communicative contexts: examples from medical encounters. In Duranti/Goodwin 1992: 291–310

Corson D J 1992 Language, gender and education: a critical review linking social justice and power *Gender and Education* 4/3: 229–54

Danet B (ed) 1984 Legal discourse *Text* 4 special issue

Deetz S 1982 Critical interpretive research in organizational communication *The Western Journal of Speech Communication* 46: 131–49

van Dijk T A 1980 *Textwissenschaft. Eine interdisziplinäre Einführung* Deutscher Taschenbuchverlag, München

van Dijk T A (ed) 1985 *Handbook of Discourse Analysis* Academic Press, New York

van Dijk T A 1989 Structures of discourse and structures of power. In J Anderson (ed) 1989 *Communication Yearbook* 12 Sage, Los Angeles: 18–59 van Dijk T A 1990 Social cognition and discourse. In H Giles, W P Robinson (eds) 1990 *Handbook of Language and Social Psychology* John Wiley and Sons, New York: 163–86

Van Dijk T A (ed) 1990 Looking ahead: discourse analysis in the 1990s. *Text* special anniversary issue **10–12**

van Dijk T A 1991 *News as Discourse* Erlbaum, Norwood

van Dijk T A 1993a *Elite Discourse and Racism* Sage, London

van Dijk T A 1993b Principles of critical discourse analysis. *Discourse and Society* **4/2**: 249–85

van Dijk T A, Kintsch W 1983 *Strategies in Text Comprehension* Academic Press, New York

Dittmar N 1973 *Soziolinguistik. Exemplarische und kritische Darstellung ihrer Theorie, Empirie und Anwendung* Fischer, Frankfurt

Dittmar N 1983 Descriptive and explanatory power of rules in sociolinguistics. In B Bain (ed) 1983 *The Sociogenesis of Language and Human Conduct* Plenum Publishing Corp, New York

Dressler W U, Merlini-Barbaresi L 1994 *Morphopragmatics. Diminutives and Intensifiers in Italian, German, and Other Languages* Mouton de Gruyter, Berlin

Dressler W U, Wodak R 1981 Sociophonological methods in the study of sociolinguistic variation in Viennese German *Language in Society* **2**: 239–70

Dressler W, Wodak R (eds) 1989 *Fachsprache und Kommunikation* Österreichischer Bundesverlag, Vienna

Drew P, Heritage J 1992 Analyzing talk at work: an introduction. In P Drew, J Heritage (eds) 1992 *Talk at work. Interaction in Institutional Settings* Cambridge University Press: 3–64

Duranti A, Goodwin C (eds) 1992 *Rethinking Context. Language as an Interactive Phenomenon* Cambridge University Press

Ehlich K 1982 'Quantitativ' oder 'qualitativ'? Bemerkungen zur Methodologiediskussion in der Diskursanalyse. In K Köhle, H Raspe (eds) 1982 *Das Gespräch während der ärztlichen Visite* Urban und Schwarzenberg, München

Ehlich K, Koerfer A, Redder A, Weingarten R (eds) 1989 *Medizinische und therapeutische Kommunikation* Westdeutscher Verlag, Opladen

Ehlich K, Rehbein J 1986 *Muster und Institution* Narr, Tübingen

Ehlich K, Switalla B 1976 Transkriptionssysteme. Eine exemplarische Übersicht *Studium Linguistik* **1**: 78–106

Eisler R (ed) 1927 *Wörterbuch der philosophischen Begriffe* Mittler, Berlin

Fairclough N 1992 *Discourse and Social Change* Polity Press

Fairclough N 1993 Critical discourse analysis and the marketization of public discourse. *Discourse and Society* **4/2**: 133–68

Fairclough N, Wodak R 1996 Critical discourse analysis. An overview. In T A van Dijk (ed) 1996 *Discourse Analysis* Sage (in print)

Farberow N 1973 Group therapy for self-destructive persons. Unpublished MS, Washington DC

Feldstein S, Brenner M, Jaffe J 1963 The effect of subject, sex, verbal interaction and topical focus on speech disruption. *Language and Speech* 2: 229–39

Ferguson C, Heath S (eds) 1981 *Language in the USA* Cambridge University Press

Fiehler R, Sucharowski W (eds) 1992 *Kommunikationsberatung und Kommunikationstraining* Westdeutscher Verlag, Opladen

Finger U D 1976 *Sprachzerstörung in Gruppen* Suhrkamp, Frankfurt

Fisher S, Groce S B 1990 Accounting Practices in Medical Interviews *Language in Society* 19: 225-50

Fisher S, Todd A D (eds) 1983 *The Social Organization of Doctor–Patient Communication* Center for Applied Linguistics, Washington

Fiske J *Understanding popular culture* Unwin Hyman, Winchester, MA

Flader D, Wodak-Leodolter R (eds) 1979 *Therapeutische Kommunikation* Scriptor, Königstein

Foucault M 1973 *Die Geburt der Klinik* Fink, München

Foucault M 1977 *The Archaeology of Knowledge* trans. A Sheridan Smith. Random House, New York

Foucault M 1979 *Discipline and Punish. The birth of prison* trans. A Sheridan Smith. Random House, New York

Foucault M 1981 *History of Sexuality* trans. R Hurley. Penguin Books

Foucault M 1990 *Archäologie des Wissens* Fischer, Frankfurt

Foucault M 1993 *Die Ordnung des Diskurses* 2nd edn trans. W Seitter. Fischer, Frankfurt

Freeman S H 1987 Organizational constraints as communicative variables in bureaucratic medical settings – A case study of patient-initated referral talk in independent practice and association-affiliated practices *Discourse Processes* 10: 385–400

Freeman S H, Heller M S (eds) 1987 Medical discourse *Text* 7 special issue

Freud S 1976 *Massenpsychologie und Ich-Analyse* (Vol. 13) Fischer, Frankfurt

Gale J E 1991 *Conversation Analysis of Therapeutic Discourse. The Pursuit of a Therapeutic Agenda* Ablex, Norwood, NJ

Gibbons J (ed) 1994 *Language and the Law* Longman

Giddens A 1979 *Central Problems in Social Theory* University of California Press, Berkeley

Giddens A 1981 *A Contemporary Critique of Historical Materialism* (Vol. 1) Macmillan

Giddens A 1982 *Profiles and Critiques in Social Theory* Macmillan

Giddens A 1988 Structuralism, post-structuralism and the production of culture. In A Giddens, J Turner (eds) 1988 *Social Theory Today* (2nd edn) Cambridge University Press: 195–223

Giddens A 1989 *Sociology* Polity Press

Goffman E 1974 *Frame Analysis* Harper and Row, New York

Goffman E 1981 *Forms of talk* Blackwell

Green H 1974 *Ich habe dir nie einen Rosengarten versprochen* Klett, Stuttgart

Gruber H 1991 *Antisemitismus im Mediendiskurs* Deutscher Universitätsverlag, Wiesbaden

Grumiller I 1975 Therapeutische Gruppenkonzepte. In H Strotzka (ed) 1975 *Psychotherapie: Grundlagen, Verfahren, Indikationen* Urban & Schwarzenberg, München

Gumperz J 1982 *Discourse Strategies* Cambridge University Press

Gumperz J J, Herasimchuk E 1972 The conversational analysis of social meaning: a study in classroom interaction. Unpublished Ms

Habermas J 1969 *Erkenntnis und Interesse* Suhrkamp, Frankfurt

Habermas J 1970a On systematically distorted communication. *Inquiry* 13: 205–18

Habermas J 1970b Towards a theory of communicative competence. *Inquiry* 13, 360–75

Habermas J 1971 Vorbereitende Bemerkungen zu einer Theorie der kommunikativen Kompetenz. In J Habermas, N Luhmann (eds) 1971 *Theorie der Gesellschaft oder Sozialtechnologie* Suhrkamp, Frankfurt

Habermas J 1975 *Legitimation Crisis* trans. T McCarthy, Beacon Press, Boston

Habermas J 1979 *Communication and the Evolution of Society* trans. T McCarthy, Beacon Press, Boston

Habermas J 1981 *Theorie des kommunikativen Handelns* Suhrkamp, Frankfurt

Habermas J 1985 *Der philosophische Diskurs der Moderne* Suhrkamp, Frankfurt

Hall S 1985 Signification, representation, ideology: Althusser and the post-structuralist debates. *Critical Studies in Mass Communication* 2: 91–114

Hardt-Mautner G 1992 *Understanding the News?* Peter Lang, Bern

Hein N 1985 Gespräche beim praktischen Arzt. MA thesis, University of Vienna

Hein N, Hoffmann-Richter U, Lalouschek J, Nowak P, Wodak R 1985 Kommunikation zwischen Arzt und Patient *Wiener Linguistische Gazette* Beiheft 4

Hein N, Wodak R 1987 Medical interviews in internal medicine *Text* 7: 37–66

Helgesen S 1990 *Frauen führen anders* Campus, Frankfurt

Heller M, Freeman S 1987 First encounters – the role of communication in the medical intake process *Discourse Processes* 10: 369–84

Helm J (ed) 1967 *Essays on the Verbal and Visual Arts* Pergamon

Hörmann H 1983 *Meinen und Verstehen. Grundzüge einer psychologischen Semantik* Suhrkamp, Frankfurt

Hymes D 1964 Introduction: toward ethnographies of communication *American Anthropologist* 6/6/2: 1–34

Kallmeyer W *et al.* 1974 *Lektürekolleg zur Textlinguistik* (Vol. 1) Athenäum, Frankfurt

Kant I 1974 *Kritik der reinen Vernunft* (first edition 1781) Suhrkamp, Frankfurt

Kintsch W, van Dijk T A 1978 Toward a model of text comprehension and production *Psychological Review* 85: 363–94

Köhle K, Raspe H (eds) 1982 *Das Gespräch während der ärztlichen Visite* Urban und Schwarzenberg, München

Kress G 1993 Against arbitrariness: the social production of the sign. *Discourse and Society* 4/2: 169–93

Kutter P 1971 Übertragung und Prozeß in der psychoanalytischen Gruppentherapie. *Psyche* 1: 856–73

Labov W 1966 *The Social Stratification of English in New York City* Center for Applied Linguistics, New York

Labov W 1969 The Logic of Nonstandard English. In Williams F (ed) 1969 *Language and Poverty* Morrow, Chicago

Labov W, Fanshel D 1977 *Therapeutic Discourse* Academic Press, New York

Labov W, Waletzky J 1967 Narrative analysis: oral versions of personal experience. In J Helm 1967: 12–44

Lakoff R T 1989 The limits of politeness: therapeutic and courtroom discourse *Multilingua* 8/2–3: 101–29

Lakoff R 1992 *Talking Power* Sage, London

Lalouschek J, Menz F, Nowak P, Wodak R 1987 *Konzept einer Gesprächsausbildung für Ärzte.* Unpublished MS, Vienna

Lalouschek J, Menz F, Wodak R 1990 *Alltag in der Ambulanz* Narr, Tübingen

Lalouschek J, Nowak P 1989 Insider-Outsider: Die Kommunikationsbarrieren der medizinischen Fachsprache. In Dressler/Wodak 1989: 6–18

Larsen S 1983 Text processing and knowledge updating in memory for radio news *Discourse Processes* 6: 21–38

Leodolter R [née Wodak] 1975a *Das Sprachverhalten von Angeklagten bei Gericht* Scriptor, Kronberg

Leodolter R [née Wodak] 1975b Gestörte Sprache oder Privatsprache: Kommunikation bei Schizophrenen. *Wiener Linguistische Gazette* 10/11: 75–95

Lorenzer A 1973 *Sprachzerstörung und Rekonstruktion* Suhrkamp, Frankfurt

Lüger H H 1983 *Pressesprache* Niemeyer, Tübingen

Lutz B 1988 Strategien des Textverstehens oder Plädoyer für einen soziopsychologischen Ansatz linguistischer Verstehensforschung PhD dissertation, University of Vienna

Lutz B, Wodak R 1987 *Information für Informierte. Linguistische Studien zu Verständlichkeit und Verstehen von Hörfunknachrichten* Verlag der Akademie der Wissenschaften, Vienna

Maas U 1988 Probleme und Traditionen der Diskursanalyse. *Zeitschrift für Phonetik, Sprachwissenschaft und Kommunikationsforschung* 41/6: 717–29

Menz F 1991 *Der geheime Dialog* Peter Lang, Bern

Minsky A 1980 A framework for representing knowledge. In D Metzing (ed) *Frame Conceptions and Text Understanding* De Gruyter, Berlin: 1–25

Mishler E G 1984 *The Discourse of Medicine. Dialectics in Medical Interviews* Ablex, Norwood, NJ

Monk R 1990 *Ludwig Wittgenstein. The Duty of Genius* Penguin Books

Moosmüller S 1989 *Studien zur Österreichischen Umgangssprache* Böhlau, Vienna

Morris Ch 1938 *Foundations of the Theory of Signs* University of Chicago Press, Chicago

Mumby D K 1988 *Communication and Power in Organizations: Discourse, Ideology and Domination* Ablex, Norwood, NJ

Pfeiffer O E, Strouhal E, Wodak R 1987 *Recht auf Sprache* Orac, Vienna

Renkeema J 1993 *Discourse Studies. An Introductory Textbook* Benjamins, Amsterdam

Roberts K H *et al.* 1977 Organization theory and organizational communication: a communication failure? *Human Relations* 27: 501–24

Russell R L 1987 Psychotherapeutic discourse: future directions and the critical pluralist attitude. In R L Russell (ed) *Language in Psychotherapy: Strategies of Discovery. Emotions, Personality, and Psychotherapy* Plenum Press, New York: 341–51

Sacks H 1986 Some considerations of a story told in ordinary conversation. MS

Schank R, Abelson R 1977 *Scripts, Plans, Goals and Understanding* Ablex, Norwood, NJ

Schegloff E A 1992 On talk and its institutional occasions. In Drew/ Heritage 1992: 101–36

Scherner M 1989 Zur kognitionswissenschaftlichen Modellierung des Textverstehens *Zeitschrift für Germanistische Linguistik* 17/1: 94–102

Schiffrin D 1993 *Approaches to Discourse* Blackwell

Schleiermacher F 1977 *Hermeneutik und Kritik* Fischer, Frankfurt

Schmidt S 1973 *Texttheorie. Probleme einer Linguistik der sprachlichen Kommunikation* Fink, München

Schneider H D 1977 *Sozialpsychologie der Machtbeziehungen* Klett, Stuttgart

Schütz A 1960 *Der sinnhafte Aufbau der sozialen Welt* Braumüller, Vienna

Searle J 1986 *Sprechakte* Suhrkamp, Frankfurt

Slater P E 1978 *Mikrokosmos: Eine Studie über Gruppendynamik* Suhrkamp, Frankfurt

Sonneck G 1976 Krisenintervention und Suizidverhütung *Ars Medici* 10: 419–24

Spranz-Fogasy T 1987 Alternativen der Gesprächseröffnung im ärztlichen Gespräch *Zeitschrift für Dialektologie und Linguistik* 15/3: 293–302

Strauss F, Sonneck G 1978 Statistische Untersuchungen über die Selbstmorde in Österreich aus den Jahren 1971–1975 *Mitteilungen der Österreichischen Sanitätsverwaltung* 4/79: 3–11

Strong P M 1979 *The Ceremonial Order of the Clinic: Parents, Doctors, and Medical Bureaucracies* Routledge and Kegan Paul, London

Strotzka H 1985 *Macht. Ein psychoanalytischer Essay* Europa Verlag, Vienna

Strotzka H, Pelikan J, Krajic K (eds) 1984 *Welche Ärzte brauchen wir? Medizinstudium und Ärzteausbildung in Österreich* Facultasverlag, Vienna

Tannen D 1990 *You Just Don't Understand. Women and Men in Conversation* Morrow, New York

Theis A M 1994 *Organisationskommunikation. Theoretische Grundlagen und empirische Forschungen* Westdeutscher Verlag, Opladen

Till W 1977 Effizienz von Krisenintervention PhD dissertation, University of Vienna

Todd A 1983 A diagnosis of doctor–patient discourse in the prescription of contraception. In Fisher/Todd 1983: 159–88

Tulving E 1972 Episodic and semantic memory. In E Tulving, W Donaldsen (eds) 1972 *Organization of Memory* Academic Press, New York: 382–403

Vass E 1992 Diskursanalyse als interdisziplinäres Forschungsgebiet. MA thesis, University of Vienna

Vogt R 1987 Zwei Modelle zur Analyse von Diskursen. In R Vogt (ed) 1987 *Über die Schwierigkeit des Verständigens beim Reden: Beiträge zur Linguistik des Diskurses* Westdeutscher Verlag, Opladen: 3–34

Warren C 1934 *Modern News Reporting* New York

Warren C 1953 *ABC des Reporters. Einführung in den praktischen Journalismus* Fink, München

Werlich E 1975 *Typologie der Texte* UTB, Heidelberg

Wessels M 1984 *Cognitive Psychology* Academic Press, New York

West C 1984 *Routine Complications. Troubles with Talk Between Doctors and Patients* Indiana University Press, Bloomington

West C 1990 Not just 'doctors' orders': directive–response sequences in patients' visits to women and men physicians. *Discourse and Society* 1/1: 85–112

Windhoff-Héritier J 1976 *Sind Frauen wie Freud sie sah?* Fischer, Frankfurt

Wittgenstein L 1967 *Philosophische Untersuchungen/Philosophical Investigations* Suhrkamp, Frankfurt trans. G E M Anscombe

Wodak R 1980 Discourse analysis and courtroom interaction *Discourse Processes* 3/4: 369–80

Wodak R 1981a Women relate, men report: sex differences in language behaviour in a therapeutic group *Journal of Pragmatics* 5: 70–93

Wodak R 1981b How do I put my problem? *Text* 1: 3–35

Wodak R 1984 Determination of guilt: discourses in the courtroom. In C Kramarae, M Schulz, W M O'Barr (eds) *Language and Power* Sage, Beverly Hills, CA: 89–100

Wodak R 1985 The interaction between judge and defendant. In van Dijk 1985 (Vol. 4): 181–93

Wodak R 1986a *Language Behavior in Therapy Groups* trans. P Smith, University of California Press, Los Angeles

Wodak R 1986b Normal and deviant texts. The sociopsychological theory of textplanning. In Y Tobin (ed) *From Sign to Text: A Semiotic View of Communication* Benjamins, Amsterdam: 333–55

Wodak R 1987a Kommunikation in Institutionen. In Ammon *et al.* 1987: 800–20

Wodak R 1987b And where is the Lebanon? A socio-psycholinguistic investigation of comprehension and intelligibility of news *Text* 7/4: 377–410

Wodak R 1989 The irrationality of power. In P Anderson (ed) 1989 *Communication Yearbook* 12 Sage, Los Angeles: 79–94

Wodak R 1992 Strategies in text production and text comprehension: a new perspective. In D Stein (ed) 1992 *Cooperating with Written Texts* Mouton, The Hague: 493–528

Wodak R 1994a Critical Discourse Analysis. In J Blommaert (ed) 1994 *Handbook of Pragmatics* Mouton, The Hague (in print)

Wodak R 1994b Critical Linguistics and the study of institutional discourse. In P Stevenson 1994 *Sociolinguistics in the German-speaking Countries* Oxford University Press (in print)

Wodak R 1994c Power, discourse and styles of female leadership in school committee meetings. In D Corson 1994 (ed) *Power and Education* (in print)

Wodak R, Andraschko E 1994 Frauen führen anders? Eine diskurssoziolinguistische Untersuchung. Teil 1 *Erziehung heute e.h.* 1: 41–9

Wodak R, Benke G 1994 Gender as a sociolinguistic variable. New perspectives on sociolinguistic variation. In F Coulmas (ed) 1994 *Sociolinguistics* Oxford University Press (in print)

Wodak *et al.* 1992 *Schulpartnerschaft – Kommunikation in der Schule* Institut für Sprachwissenschaft, Projectreport, Vienna

Wodak R, Lutz B 1986 Ein Amerikaner in China. Nachrichten als Fortsetzungsroman *Medien Journal* 4: 202–7

Wodak R, Menz F, Lalouschek J 1989 *Sprachbarrieren. Die Verständigungskrise der Gesellschaft* Edition Atelier, Vienna

Wodak R, Moosmüller S, Doleschal U, Feistritzer G 1987 *Sprachliche Gleichbehandlung von Frau und Mann* Ministry for Social Affairs, Vienna

Wodak R, Nowak P, Pelikan J, Gruber H, de Cillia R, Mitten R 1990 *'Wir sind alle unschuldige Täter' Diskurshistorische Studien zum Nachkriegsantisemitismus* Suhrkamp, Frankfurt

Wodak R, Schulz M 1986 *The Language of Love and Guilt* Benjamin, Amsterdam

Wodak R, van de Craen P (eds) 1987 *Neurotic and psychotic Language Behaviour* Multilingual Matters

Wodak-Leodolter R 1977 Interaktion in einer therapeutischen Gruppe: eine soziolinguistische Analyse *Wiener Linguistische Gazette* 15: 33–60

Wodak-Leodolter R, Dressler W U 1978 Phonological variation in colloquial Viennese *Michigan Germanic Studies* 4/1: 30–66

Index